Keeping the Faith Through

Life's Greatest Battles

BY
JESSICA SHELTON

Copyright ©2020 Jessica Shelton

All rights reserved. No part of this publication may be reproduced, distributed, or transmitted in any form or by any means, including photocopying, recording, or other electronic or mechanical methods, without the prior written permission of the publisher, except in the case of brief quotations embodied in critical reviews and certain other noncommercial uses permitted by copyright law.

ISBN-978-1-951300-17-3

Liberation's Publishing – West Point - Mississippi

Keeping the Faith Through

Life's Greatest Battles

BY
JESSICA SHELTON

Keeping the Faith Through Life's Greatest Battles

Table of Content

Intro 7

A letter To My husband 9

Grief 11

Healing 21

The Second Blow 29

Coping.. 43

Thoughts from My Husband 55

When It's All Said and Done 61

In Honor of BLM.. 63

Intro

Well hello there! Before I start to tell you my truth, I want to introduce myself. My name is Jessica. I have two wonderful kids a boy and a girl and a loving devoted hardworking husband. I am truly blessed to have my little family. Well now that I have introduced myself, I want to let you know no you didn't buy this book by accident. There's a reason, and I hope while you read all about my truth some of these words are able to touch your soul or heal your broken heart. My reason for writing this book is to show you that you are not alone in your fight. Just like myself many have battled with the same feelings of doubt, fear, and hurt.

Keeping the Faith Through Life's Greatest Battles

Jessica Shelton

A Letter To My Husband

I remember blushing every time you called. (first guy I really liked). I remember getting overly excited when you said to get dressed because you wanted to take me out (didn't ask me for nothing just wanted to see me). I remember our first Valentines 😊. You gave me my first bouquet flowers and a big box of chocolate (we were only seventeen). I remember when I got sick and lost my voice. You called my aunt and told her you were coming to bring me something to make me feel better. When you came to drop it off you hugged me and game me a kiss on the forehead.

I remember when I was nineteen and our house burned down you told me whatever I needed you were there. I remember when we got our new house and we were still getting situated, you found out that I had no bed. Even though I told you it was coming, I saw the look in your eyes. You left and I remember thinking, this was too much for you to deal with. I felt my heart breaking because I started to think the worse. That's what anxiety will do to you.

Two hours later you came back wit a couple

of bags. It was clothes and shoes. Wow! All for me. Then you said, "I have one more thing for you." You brought in a queen-sized blow-up mattress and said, "It's not much but I understand."

My heart wanted to burst from all of the love that was in that. I remember us growing up together but falling more and more in love as we grew together. I remember the day we got married. How extremely happy we were to finally be as one. I remember working hard together and buying a home. Us saying we would build our empire.

I also remember five years into the marriage getting hit with the news that I had cancer. I remember all my scares and fears. I remember my hair fell out and thinking you were going to leave. Instead you shaved your head bald and said, "We are in this for the long haul."

Oh yeah boy how I remember!

Love Jessica

Grief

Everyone deals with grief in their own way. We cry, we get angry, we eat, we sleep etc. One thing we can all agree on is that we hate it when people try to tell us how to grieve, or how long to grieve. Let me tell you about when I lost my mom. I want to tell you about her, because hey! It's my truth. My mom had been sick for quite some time. My family and I always had faith that my mom, my best friend, could and would pull through. I mean come on she went to church all the time. She even made sure we were there dressed in our Sunday best. She raised us with very strong values as I'm sure you guys parents (loved ones) did the same.

I mean she made sure we were showing respect to our elders, putting God first, treating others the way we want to be treated. My favorite word to live by "if you help someone the world doesn't have to know that's between you and them." She was a very smart caring and intelligent individual. She never for one moment made us doubt her love for us. She was the perfect mom.

Growing up I never needed or wanted for a friend because she was it. I never hungered for love because she poured all she had into us. Everything I ever did in school she made sure she was involved in as well. No matter how sick or how much pain she was in, she made sure she showed us to support. When I was sad or sick, she was right there being the best mom she could be. I knew I could always count on her.

Not to mention when I got pregnant with my daughter, she was so excited. I think if it was possible, she would've been more thrilled than I was. Throughout my pregnancy I had some complications, which caused us all to fear. One thing I knew my mom wasn't leaving my side. She would always put herself last. During my labor (sixteen and a half hours) of pure pain, they came to tell me if I continue to try to have my daughter naturally, I wouldn't make it. They needed to do C-section I looked at my husband, then my mom. My mom reassured me that I was stronger than I thought. Plus, she'd be waiting and praying. God had us and needless to say everything worked out perfectly. Our healthy baby girl was born in two thousand eleven. My mom was most definitely my prayer warrior; my backbone I knew I could count on her and her prayers.

Okay, we are going to fast forward a couple months to the time when my baby girl had her first major seizure. I at the time didn't know what to do. I didn't even know what was happening. I did know we needed God and my mom. Can you imagine being a first-time parent; jumping out of your bed to see your baby's lips purple, eyes rolled back, feeling hotter than a car's engine.

We don't have to imagine because, honey, we were living it. All I could do was cry out and call on God. My husband put her in water to cool her off. The police and ambulance arrived, and I called my mom. I had so many tears running down my face. Of course, like always she was right there. by my side to hold my hand and pray. It always seemed to make things better when she prayed. While we were there in the hospital room not knowing the outcome, my mom had her back turned to us. My baby's hand started to move and a couple of minutes later her eyes opened. All I could do was cry with relief and hug my mom and husband.

Matthew 17:20, "Jesus said to them, "Because of your unbelief; for assuredly, I say to you, if you have faith as a mustard seed, you will say to this mountain, 'Move from here to there,' and it will move; and nothing will be impossible for you."

Now my reason for telling you that story is so you can see just how devoted of a mother she truly was. So after about a year of going through it with baby girl the seizures finally calmed down. Who would have thought shortly after my angel (my mom) would be taken from me? My mom that is.

That Sunday I was to get up and make my way to the hospital to have breakfast with her. When I was stopped immediately by my husband. I didn't know what he could have possibly wanted. I mean what could have been so important that he was willing to have me late for a date with my mom? That's what I'm thinking. As quick as I had that thought I paid attention to him. He had the look of hurt and pain on his face. He then started to tell me that the most important person in my life, my best friend, my first heart, the person I spent my days with, talked to about everything with, was no longer my here.

My heart now felt as though it was in my throat. I started to feel numb but hurt, angry, and disappointed. How can this be true? How could the woman who's been my whole world possibly be gone? What were, my brothers, myself, and omg my dad going to do? She's everything to us. What was happening? I asked, "God can you please explain this part of life? Do you really know what you just did? Do you know you just turned our world upside down?

Why did he take my angel? What could our God almighty have been thinking? Didn't he know I still needed her? Not only me; but my dad and my brothers. My youngest brother was only thirteen at the time. At the same time that these thoughts and questions where running through my mind, I was running into the hospital.

As I was walking down the hall to see my mom's lifeless body for the last time. It seemed to be the longest walk of my life. My body seemed as though it wanted to collapse. I see all of my family gathered around. They are talking, but I hear any words. You know you watch these movies, and you see the part where they are there, and things are moving in slow motion. The words of people are muffled. That was me at that moment. I was watching this this unreal scene unfold.

Anger began to settle in. All the while one of my aunts was telling me to stay calm. "It's all ok?" Who was she to say such a thing? She wasn't feeling this pain. Yes, it was her sister, but my hurt was entirely different. She had no right. I no longer wanted this connection with any of them. and why should I. This God that I've been praying to can come and take them from me. For him to not hold up his end of the deal. I mean I did what our father in heaven told me to do. I fasted, I prayed, and I went to church. He told me if I asked, I shall receive. I did just that and now look. He still took my mom. "I did what you said, and you still turned your back on me. You let me down."

A week had pasted, and I was looking at my heart laying in a metal box. Everyone was coming around looking at her like she was on display. I could think of a lot of other people who deserved to be laying up there other than her. As I sat and there and listened to the preacher, I couldn't help but wonder, "God why were you putting my soul through this hurt? Why didn't you answer me? What was the purpose of this pain? I'm now in a dark place, and Lord I don't see my way out.

I'm trying my best to push my family away. No one is listening! Why don't they understand I'm done? I don't want to be close anymore. Plus, God has stopped listening. If he were truly listening my angel would still be here living life with me. But no! Where was she? Six feet under. What kind of God would take such a beautiful soul? There were sex traffickers, drug dealers, liars, and God knows who else, still running around living life.

Now I'm stuck with questions. Like did he pull the wrong number. Because surely her number couldn't really be up. Did I not pray hard enough? What did I do wrong? I promise if you do a miracle and bring her back, I'll do better. You know what? Never mind. How about I just stop going to church. How about I stop praying and stop loving. Clearly this God that's supposed to love me has truly turned his back on me. All wrong thoughts to have, I know.

Weeks later after the laying my mom to rest, I was lying in bed tossing and turning. I mean I just couldn't get comfortable. I couldn't sleep and as clear as day I hear

"You prayed and she prayed. She prayed for relief whether it be on this side or the other. Why would you want to keep her here on earth dealing pain and struggling to keep a smile on her face; to hide her true feelings. "You asked why I didn't take somebody else and leave your mother I take those that are ready so others I leave have a chance to get ready. Remember I'll always be here for you through your anger and pain when you lose sight of your purpose. My good child I never turned a deaf ear to your prayer. I heard every word and saw every tear, and I was there to wipe them. Listen I'll be your mother your friend and your God you'll never need. So, get up and hold your head up, because you have a life to live. And listen she was never yours; she was always mine you were just borrowing one of my many angels. I thought so much of you and your brothers that I decided to let you 'all experience a real-life angel."

Hebrew 11:1 "Now faith is the substance of things hoped for, the evidence of things not seen."

John 14:27 "27 Peace I leave with you, my peace I give unto you: not as the world giveth, give I unto you. Let not your heart be troubled, neither let it be afraid."

Healing

A month after losing my mom, I find out I'm six weeks pregnant. Yes, you read that right. Pregnant! So now there's so many different feelings going on inside of my head. On one hand, "Yay!" I'd always wanted two kids. On the other hand, "Holy crap! I just buried a piece of my heart. I'm still grieving. My heat is having so many conflicting feelings. It's broken but happy.

I'm thanking God but also mad at him. I tell myself get it together girl, because you now have a life brewing inside of you. This is now another little piece of happiness after the storm. Plus, you don't have time to wallow. Your daughter is looking to you to be strong for her. And let's not forget your thirteen-year old brother. Yeah! Crazy for me to forget the fact that you have family members who are willing to be there and hold your hand. They were there to show you that they care and that you were not alone.

You also have a loving devoted husband who never once left your side. He told you every morning that the two of you would get through this together. Let's face it people sometimes we feel like no-one cares or understands. Even though they say they do, we feel like no one has our back. We feel like God almighty has turned his back on us. Even though he tells us over and over in the bible maybe about over one hundred times that he'll never leave us nor forsake us.

At that moment we are not thinking we are feeling strong with emotions. It has went straight passed you. Not only did you lose your mother, but so did your brothers. You, you have just been blessed with a wonderful gift. That my friend is bringing another life into this world to love and protect. So put your big girl panties on and start loving the crap out of your daughter and take care of yourself so you can take care of that unborn child that you've been blessed with.

Cool uh nothing else can go wrong right? Oh,

my friends how wrong you and me both can be. So, let's fast forward some months. I am now eight months pregnant. Yeah very close to having my sweet baby boy. I'm home cooking getting ready for my husband to come walking through the door. Once he does walk in something is wrong. I can tell. What is it now? Its written all over his face.

He comes in and tells me to sit down. he needs to talk to me. We walk into the living room to have the most awkward conversation ever. He looks me into my eyes and tells me that he's being let go from his job. I give him a hug and tell him we'll get through. All the long I'm thinking how is this possible. I mean how are we going to get through this. We have a child to take care of and one on the way. While I was deep in thought he kneeled down before me and told me not to worry because he was going to take care of his family with the help of God.

One thing I love about my husband is, he knows, and he never forgets that God is always in control. So, the next week I go to file for government assistance and I felt so bad. How did we go from not needing anyone to needing government assistance? The only income that was coming in would be his unemployment check which would only be two-hundred-thirty dollars. As I sit in the waiting room waiting to be called back, all I could think about was what was the purpose of going through this do?

I reasoned, "God do you not see we have a child and one on the way?" Why would he take away the only income we have? Shhhh! This is some crazy stuff, but what could I do besides pray anyway. Here comes the lady to call us to the back. I was told I would have to answer a whole lot of personal questions, so before she could even begin, I started talking. I told her that my husband was the sole provider of our family. The only income we had coming in was supposed to be his unemployment which would be about two-hundred and thirty dollars. It was going to be taxed.

She explained to me that they went by gross income. I was shocked. I'm like, "that's not what he's bringing in." Anyway. When it was all said and done, she looks at me and says, "I've calculated all your expenses, and it shows that you are eligible for assistance. We'll be giving you forty dollars a month. Wow! What are we supposed to do with that? It's a good thing that we had paid up our bills. We had a savings account. I mean come on now. Who can really live off of two-hundred dollars a week? Are you serious?

Yes, of course I'm scared, hurt, and angry. I didn't know what to do. It felt as though God just kept leaving me to hang. As my daughter and I existed the building. I looked down at her and I began to pray.

"Lord I know you helped my husband and I create this family. Now we need you to continue to help us provide for this family. Lord we are depending on you"

I tell my husband what was said at the

assistance office. I tell him, "babe we are going to be ok. God does everything for a reason. He hears all and he sees all. We just got to keep the faith." I say all this all while thinking to myself, "how is it that I'm telling him this while having a hard time believing myself." Let me tell you it was a constant battle.

As I continued to pray and try my best not to question God another blow struck. We get a letter in the mail stating that my husband wasn't going to get unemployment. I take that up to the assistance office. We get the help we needed.

My husband hadn't yet found a job, so he took a job cutting a lady's yard in an upscale neighborhood. He was cutting her yard and bringing in enough money to pay our mortgage. To my surprise the lady would constantly tell me that God told her to do something extra for our family. The extra that she did allowed us to be able to pay the rest of our bills.

No. I never once told her what we were going

through. She said she had been praying to God to send her a nice family that she could help. She said that when she saw my husband her heart gravitated towards him. All I could do was smile because I knew that it was all because of God. I knew he had set this up. Yes, I worried I'm only human. My husband ended up working for her for about a month before he found a nice job with benefits. Wouldn't you know it? Right after he found that job the lady that was put in our path to help us died. It was right before the new year came in.

My heart was sad and a little broken. I was happy that I was able to share stories with her. I loved that my kids and I were able to keep her company while my husband did her yard. Before God called her home, she was happy and helping. I knew that God had one more task for her to do before he took her. Be our angel. "Ain't that something!" God is always on time.

I mean I had always heard of God doing

things like that. Here I was being a living witness to one of his many miracles. I will never understand why God does the things he does, but I can say I'm absolutely thrilled that God allowed me to experience having this angel in my life.

Psalm 130:5 "5 I wait for the Lord, my soul doth wait, and in his word do, I hope.

Psalm 9:18 "For the needy shall not always be forgotten: the expectation of the poor shall not perish forever.

The Second Blow

So here it is about a year later and we are getting ready for my son's 1st birthday party. I've got everything together, invitations, decorations, food, and presents. I'm preparing everything making sure it's perfect for my prince. I start to put up his decorations and suddenly feel this sharp pain shooting in my chest. It hurts so bad it takes my breath away. You know mothers. I don't have time to worry about me right now. That's what I thought.

It's my big boy's birthday. It's time to have some fun. As the day goes on, I start to feel this pain more and more. I go to a family member to tell them what's going on just to basically be told, "It's nothing. Brush it off. I was being dramatic." So, I did just that. I couldn't really enjoy myself the way I wanted to because the pain was hitting harder. I wanted to confide in someone. But I thought that the next person I told might feel the same way as the other. I was being dramatic.

I ended up cutting the party short, so I could go to the ER. I sat and waited for someone to come tell me why I was in so much pain. I mean really come on. We all know it's not normal for a person to be hurting so bad that their oxygen is being cut off.

The doctor assistant finally decided to show their face, and guess what they said? They said to me that everything was normal. There wasn't anything there. Take some muscle relaxers and loose a little weight. I mean I could agree with them. I needed to drop a few pounds, but I didn't agree that there wasn't anything going on. There wasn't much else I could do right then.

They had instructed and lose weight. I started on my journey to lose weight. I got more active and cut all the junk out. As time went on the pain got worse. My husband took me to another doctor in another city. Still I was told the same thing. Y'all at this time I had done seen over three different doctors. It was costing us hundreds of dollars. To have no one believe that something was going.

As time went on and the kids got a little older, I started working this little restaurant job. It was great in the beginning then all of a sudden pain shot through my chest harder than ever. It brought me straight to my knees. All I could do was cry out to God to fix whatever was going on with me. I couldn't do it, and these doctors didn't know what was happening.

After work I went home and explained to my husband what had happened at work. He asked me what I wanted to do. Did I want to quit or just find another doctor? He was out of answers, and so were the doctors I had been seeing. As I sat and thought about it some more, it came to me to try a little harder to lose weight. That's what we did. We both hit it harder than ever. It was not only to look better but feel better also.

We could make sure we were going to be here for our little ones. As we all know no one loves or cares for your kids like you. On Saturday we decided to ride our bikes to my aunt's house. It was like one and a half to two miles. As we make it to her house I pass out on her floor from pain. Her daughter ask was I ok. We laughed and I said yeah I was probably just overweight that's all."

In the back of my mind I knew that something horrific was happening to me. I couldn't tell them. I mean why would I? There was nothing they could do. If they could, would they even believe me? As I lay on her floor to rest for a minute, I decided to put on my big girl pants and head back home without saying a word to anybody. Guys by the time I made it in front of my house I was out of breath and hurting so bad I couldn't breathe.

On that note we were headed back to the hospital. X rays were done, but again there was nothing, so they said. I sat there in that bed holding my kids while I held my husband's hand. I cried because I knew something was wrong. I felt like they just didn't care. It wasn't them someone they loved. What was I to do? I couldn't afford to go up north to find a better doctor. All I could do was call on the best doctor I knew, and that was God. I needed him like never before.

We made it home, ordered Chinese, and decided to call it a night. After a few hours of just lying in bed staring at the ceiling I was finally able to fall asleep. For some reason I was awaken very early that Sunday morning. I saw my phone ringing. And yes, I said saw. I had put my phone on silent before I fell asleep. I needed time alone. It was my grandma calling to tell me that a doctor from the ER had been trying to reach me.

As I hurried off the phone with her to give this doctor a call back. My heart was in my stomach. I sat up in my bed and called the ER doctor. I was so nervous. I could have thrown up. After asking to speak to the doctor I hear a voice say,

"Hello is this Mrs. Jessica Shelton?"

"Yes, it is." I say to him.

He tells me his name and goes on to inform me that there was a 6 cm ball sitting right in the middle of my chest. At that moment I felt both relieved and scared. Scared because, OMG! what could this be. I mean my dad side has a history of cancer. I was relieved because omg I knew I wasn't crazy. As I tuned back into the conversation, I hear him say that they were supposed to put my Xray up, but for some reason it was left out on the table. He needed me to go see a certain doctor, so they could now get to the bottom of what was happening to me. He went on to say he would set my appt for three days from this time.

Here we are at the appointment waiting to see what's about to happen. As she comes in and sits down, she tells us that they are going to have to set up a biopsy. They had to see if the tumor in my chest was cancerous or not. They would begin this process within a week.

Three weeks later we were called back into her office. Once again, we're sitting and waiting with our heads bowed in prayer. Family members were awaiting my call as soon as I found out any news. As the door creaked open, I feel a lump in my throat. She comes in; sits and looks at me and starts to ask me questions about everyone except me. In my mind I'm like, "please come on, because I can't take this anymore." Just as I thought it, she leaned over to me and said, "Mrs. Shelton, I'm sorry to have to tell you this, but you have one of the rarest forms of cancer to ever hit the us. It's called Thymic cancer. There have only been ninety-nine cases before you. Mrs. Shelton you make case number one hundred.

She began to tell me all the things they planned to do. For starters surgery radiation and hopefully there would be no chemo involved. She would call me with some dates. Now how is it out of all the things I could possibly get, I end up with a rare cancer. Lord what are we about to do? I place my hands on my head.

A couple of weeks later, she called and said

that the surgery will be the first thing they perform. She told me that the surgery would take ten to eleven hours, and that I had a week to prepare.

We work on getting all of our things in order. A week later we headed out of town to the appointed surgery. While loading up bags in the car, I get calls from my dad, grandma, pastor, and cousins. They say that they are coming to be with us. I reminded them that the surgery would take ten to eleven hours, but they all assured me that no matter how long it took, they were going to be there.

I smiled the biggest smile. Even with all those people standing by me, I still felt like I was completely alone. It terrified me. I was determined to live no matter what. After all, when they finished the surgery, I would be free of this cancer. I would be on my way to recovery, or so I thought.

Thirteen hours later, they wheeled me out so that my family could see me. I was so happy to see them. I was thanking God that I made it through the surgery. All of a sudden, I hear my husband on the phone with his brother saying that they couldn't get tumor out because it had too many vessels running through it. They had nicked one of the vessels trying to get it out. I immediately started to cry because this was my chance to be free. Why didn't it work?

So, after two and a half weeks in the hospital I was able to come home. I came home to quite a surprise. My dear friend Meg had gathered with a lot of other people and gave my family one heck of a Christmas. I mean my grandmother was delivering presents for about a week. Meg stated that they all decided that this was their way of easing my and my husband's mind.

There were so many gifts coming that I actually started blessing other families. I shed so many tears, because I couldn't believe the outpour of kindness that was shown to me and my family. Malachi 3:10 says, "if I will not open you the windows of heaven, and pour you out a blessing, that there shall not be room to receive it."

Now after I healed good enough, I was sent to do seventy rounds of radiation. While doing those rounds my throat closed on me. I wasn't able to eat a thing and sometimes not even swallow my own spit. I knew I had to keep my faith and push to live. People may think there's nothing to that radiation thing. Baby that itself is a rough thing. I went every day for about three or four months, and I did get weary. I kept telling myself your babies need you to push.

When you find yourself in a situation like this you have to find your reason. If you can't just think God needs, you to testify to someone else. After the radiation treatments I went on to chemo. And yes! I thought I was about to blow through this thing with a breeze just like I did with radiation. Let me tell you I was in for a ride. Awakening my first month didn't seem so bad. I was just weak, and I had no appetite. All in all, I felt I was ok. The months after that was something awful.

And no. I didn't tell my folks what was going on with me. I would smile and say, "I'm alright." In reality there were times where I couldn't stop myself from vomiting. My sides, my stomach, my chest, everything would cramp up so bad. I would get so weak I could barely stand.

There was this one time that I was in the ER. I couldn't stop vomiting. The nurse that tried to help me kept telling the doctor she couldn't help me because I was vomiting to violently. That night I thought God was calling me home. While I was going through it all I kept telling myself, "I shall live and not die."

God hadn't given me these kids to call me home early. While I lay in that bed with tubes running all over my body, I actually had thoughts of throwing in the towel. I knew that wasn't an option. I know what some may think, "Oh she's got so much support. She's good." It's different when you are the one going through it. You think of ending your life just to be out of pain. You think anything is better than going through what you are going through at that moment. By the time I reached my seventh round of Chemo, I was pleading with my doctor to let God take control. "Just please no more chemo."

I didn't feel I could take anymore. So, after my pleading she agreed to let me take a break. After going back to my appointments, a couple times to check on the tumor and cancer she was amazed to see that it was still there. It sat there on the left side beside my heart not moving but staying put. She looked me in my eyes and said she didn't understand what was happening. She had never seen anything like this before. She had to be honest with me. She stated how when I first came to her she didn't think I was going to make it.

Nevertheless, she went on to say. "As long as the tumor didn't grow, she would leave me off chemo. I smiled and said, "as long as you got God in the mix what man think is impossible God will make possible. If God wanted me to live with a tumor in my chest, I'll take. Just as long as I'm still here.

Keeping the Faith Through Life's Greatest Battles

Coping

See what's crazy is people seem to always think they know more about a sickness than the person that's actually going through it. Each person's experience is different. Even if you read about it to get a better understanding, you'll never truly understand.

Throughout the time I've been going through cancer some of the things I went through was pretty scary to me. There were times when I didn't know if I was going to live or die. Some of those things made me physically and mentally drained. I tried my best not to complain and to seem as strong as I possibly could for my family.

I didn't want my kids to worry about anything. They were young, and we as adults think they don't understand. that's the biggest lie we can tell ourselves. Their mood changes just like ours. Any who... I also tried my best to seem as normal as possible when my husband was home, because I didn't want him worrying either. I mean, he already had enough on his plate. He'd be at work worrying about me and wouldn't be as focused as he needed to be. That would cause him to not be safe. So, I tried as best I could to hide the way I was feeling. I felt as though I may have been a burden to him, as well as the rest of my family.

That's why every time the question came up, "How are you feeling? or Do you need anything?" came up, my answer was and is I'm fine or no I don't need anything. Honestly deep down I felt and sometimes still feel as though I'm drowning inside wishing that I could let them know that I really feel. Sometimes it's like I'm lost, and no one really and truly understands. Even if I told them it wouldn't be the same.

To know that some of them {family} feel like it's a put on, a show, a cry for attention. I eat it or stay away from them. When I'm depressed or stressed, I go through alone. Who's going to really understand. I even went through a period when I thought it would be easier if I ended it.

When I was doing chemo, I experienced some really rough things one of the toughest things I went through was losing my hair. Another was vomiting. When I was told that I was going to lose my hair, I thought well it won't be that bad on me. It's just hair, but OMG! Was I wrong! I was in the shower washing my hair when I realized I was getting clumps of my hair in my hands. Seeing my hair come out you would think, "OMG! She's about to freak out." But no, it didn't hit me until I looked in the mirror while combing my hair.

I saw patches missing. So, I immediately told my husband that we needed to go ahead and cut my hair. I didn't think it would bring me to tears, because like I said its only hair. As soon as I saw the hair hit the floor, my eyes started to water. I mean y'all I tried as hard as I could to stay strong and not show emotions. I wanted to show my kids as well as my husband that it wasn't bothering me.

It really was. It wasn't just the hair. No. It was the fact that reality had sunk in. I was going through a major sickness that many had died from.

My heart felt like it was breaking all over again. When he was finally finished cutting my hair, I went to look in the mirror. While looking I heard the clippers start again. OMG! Would you believe it. My hubby, my best friend in all the world was cutting his hair just to make me feel better. Yes. It did help a little.

During the day I was okay. At night, as I lay in bed while everyone else slept, I was there alone with my thoughts which scared me. It was the not knowing what was to come of this. Was I going to survive? Was I going to be left with a lifetime illness where I'd need a nurse? Was my husband going to grow tired of me and walk away? Was God punishing me for something I may have done in another life?

I had so many other thoughts that I held inside. I know reading this, many people will think, "How is it that she still felt alone when people by her side helping her through? Why is she holding so much in? Why won't she let them in to help take the load off? They're there. All she had to do was use them."

Well let me tell you my friends. That's easier said than done. Like I said before the thoughts are what keep people from receiving the help that's right there in front of them. You start to think that the people who are there to help really don't want to help. They are there to be nosey. They just want something to talk about. They don't truly honestly care about you. Just as soon as they help you, they'll be off to tell the next person what they did.

So, of course like many others. I held it in even though I truly needed them. When my family came over to help me with simple tasks, I would tell them it's ok. Me and my husband had it crazy ain't it? Why not accept the help that's being offered to you? Like I said the mind is truly a piece of work. That person coming over to offer help could have easily taken the load off me as well as my husband.

My husband would work a full shift then come home and clean the kitchen. I mean after dealing with people all day and then have to come home and deal with more. I mean what was I supposed to do. What I started doing was holding on to the walls of my house and taking it upon myself to handle things that needed to be handled. Of course, I'm not going to call anyone. Why? So, they can talk. I wasn't about to give them the ammo. They're looking for family or not those people don't truly care.

This is what goes on in a person's head. They suffer with some sort of anxiety in silence. So, I chose to not let the ones in that cared the most about me. It's a shame isn't it? To go through something and have all the help that you could possibly want and still feel like God left you here to suffer alone.

Later on, during my chemo treatments, I developed severe vomiting. On this particular day, my husband decided to cook himself. I was shocked, because let's face it in all the years we had been together I had never seen him cook. Lol mostly because I felt it was my job. My job to have food on the table rather he was working or not. I didn't want his hands to touch my kitchen. That was my place. Anyway, there he was all 5 feet 11 inches of a man in my kitchen cooking us a meal. He had decided to cook spaghetti and fish.

While I was laid up on the couch {I didn't do much laying in my room because I couldn't see my family}. He handed me a plate. I tried to get him to take it back because I had no appetite. One thing he would always say to me to get me to eat was, "baby you are not fighting to stay here with us if you don't at least try to eat." So, I took the plate, and I took a bite even though I couldn't taste or smell the food.

Oh yeah! Did I tell you going through this had done took my sense of taste and smell? I've been off chemo for two years and I still can barely taste or smell. While I was trying my best to eat a little bit of what he cooked, it immediately turned my stomach upside down. As he helped me to the bathroom to throw up, I caught a glance of sadness on his face. I continued to throw up. He went to deal with the kids.

I kid you not! I stayed with my head in the toilet for at least twenty-minutes. As I continued to throw up green sour stuff, my body started to cramp up. I couldn't stop the vomiting and I struggled to tell him that I really need to go to the ER.

As he rushed me there, I still was unable to talk to him because I was yet throwing up and cramping. I started to panic. Yeah! In the middle of all this I'm now having a panic attack. Once at the ER, they were finally able to stop me from vomiting. That was one of the scariest things I'd ever went through, because I didn't know what was about to happen to me.

I did know what to do and that was pray. When I was finally about to sit back, they pumped fluids back into my body. I looked over at my husband and kids. There was the look of stress, concern, and hurt all rolled into one. That's when I thought was me fighting to be here really worth it.

Am I hurting them more dragging them through this with me? Would it be better if I stopped it all and just let nature take its course? What could I do to stop the hurt I thought I was inflicting on them?

It hit me. "Girl are you crazy? No one can love them the way you do. No one can or will show them care like you. Who's going to show them how to be strong. You need to pull it together and stop with the pity party. Show your babies what being strong is. That day is the day I decided to fight and fight like my kid's life depended on it. If I wasn't going to live for me, I most definitely needed to live for them.

I reached deep within myself to find strength I never knew was there. I battled and have battled with mental and physical sickness pain in my body that only God knows where its coming from. See, when a person goes through something like cancer not only are they going through physically, they go through mentally. Their body goes through but their mind too. Yes. We think about ending our life because it's freaking exhausting.

You have to deal with some loved ones thinking you're all a show. They think you just want attention. You find yourself praying that God would allow them to spend at least one day in your body, one day having your mind. Let's see how they'd handle being you.

Those of you who think a person going through wants your attention, you may be right they. Do they want you to see that they need you? They want you to understand. They want you to hold their hand through this. When you go to sleep pain free, thought free, sick free, they are going to bed still dealing with it all.

I asked God, "Why I had to gotten cut on? Why I had to go through chemo and radiation? Why I had to suffer the burns, my throat closing on me where I couldn't eat for days. The pain of why I had to sit for eight hours on a machine that pumped poison through my body. It caused me not to be able to eat sleep or play with my kids for weeks at a time. At the same time being grateful that I had three good days before I had to start all over again.

I would always and pray that this time won't be as bad as the last. At least I could get my body used to the hell its going through. Why I had to go through something so traumatic? It may have caused me not to be able to bring forth another life. Why was it that my husband and I weren't able to have a healthy sex life? We feared that it could or would cause problems with his health. Why did my kids have to see mommy so sick? They had to wonder if mommy was going to have to live with grandma in heaven. How would my husband or I answer the questions when we both wondered the same thing?

One may think it was easier because I had a spouse, but you have to think about what we went through.

Keeping the Faith Through Life's Greatest Battles

Thoughts from My Husband

When I was going through chemo treatment not only did, I think about what I was going through, I thought about my "boo thang" as well. (Did y'all see that my BOO THANG lol.) I would constantly ask him how he was feeling. Did he want to talk? His reply would always be, "don't worry about me. I'm ok." For the longest of time he wouldn't talk to me about it no matter how much or often I would ask him. He chose to work out his frustration through doing yard work or working on the cars.

I really just started finding these things out. He would just drown himself in work instead of talking it through with me. It was really taking a toll on our marriage. He wasn't talking and neither one of us as I said before knew what was going to happen. I didn't have life insurance because prior to us trying to get it, I was told I had cancer. That stopped it.

Even now I'm put on a let's wait and see list

because of the cancer. Not only was he worried about my health, now he was stuck with what would be left once and if I passed on. He thought, "if the person I love and fell in love with dies, how am I going to bury her." Not only will he be in the midst of grieving, he would be left with this huge burden.

As I stated before he chose to bury himself in work, so that he wouldn't have to think about what we were going through. Any time I brought up the situation it started an argument between us. He felt talking wouldn't make things better.

After years of asking him how he was feeling and trying my best to get him to talk to me he finally came to confided in me. He told me that it was the hardest thing that he had ever went through in his life. He had felt so helpless seeing the woman that he loved go through something that was out of both our hands. He said that throughout life he was able to control everything and make the outcome be what he wanted it to be. For the first time it was beyond him and this was something he couldn't fix.

Him being the man he was, felt at a loss. He felt helpless as a newborn baby. He said some nights he would sit in bed at night and watch me sleep. He would beg God not to take me from them. Not only did the kids need me, so did he. He said that so many times he wished that he could fix what was going on in my body like he did when it came to the cars. Now he was having to depend on a doctor he didn't know to fix what he wanted most in the world.

Yes, ladies and gentlemen while I interviewed my husband for this book, I blushed more than a fourteen-year-old schoolgirl. He had become totally dependent. One reason he didn't want to talk about it before is that he didn't want to stress me out. He let it be known that he now found himself praying harder and more than he ever had before. He found himself loving me harder, wanting to hold me longer, wanting to go and do things more as a family. He found himself thanking God more and falling in love with me all over again.

Awe. Sweet aint it? Yes, yes, yes, it is. He also said that at certain times during all of this he felt as though it was too much. Let's be honest. I too felt it was too much. Neither one of us knew what to do. Do you want to know who did? God did. He had an old Ram in the bush. Our marriage felt as though it had grown stronger. Our faith in God was stronger.

We had a testimony that I felt needed to be reached by many. Yes, I am going through somethings, but let's take a gander. I am in early remission from a cancer my doctor calls rare. She said that out of all the people to get this rarity I made case number **100**. That means that there hasn't been a lot of time spent studying this cancer. LOL. God chose little old me to take on such a sickness and show the world that even when faced with a thing such as this, he's still God almighty.

He can and will show up and show his mighty muscles and show the world that he's still capable of doing what man finds impossible. Yeah, I know throughout this book I questioned God. My faith was shaking. You want to know something, even though I am on the better end of this sickness there will probably still be times I question or have my faith will be shaken a little. As long as I we remember that God has the upper hand, he is and will forever be in control. We also got to realize that when we go through, even though we feel alone, we are not alone. We have people ready and willing to listen. Even if your family turns a deaf ear to you there are counselors there at the hospitals ready to lend their ear.

I know it's hard to get out of our own way, but you have to. We are the authors of our own stories. No one can tell your story like you. Through all of your hurt pain and anger you have to find the courage to still move forward. No matter how bad or unfair life may seem, remember God made you in all of his image.

When It's All Said and Done

I will say this, even with a huge support system, thoughts of dying will cross your mind. I want to tell you, I found myself standing there holding all of my meds in my hands while others were sleeping. I thought about it and remembered some are falling into depression, having anxiety attacks, or loosing loved one, reach a little deeper.

Pray a little harder get on your knees and cry out to the almighty living God. He'll give you strength that you never thought you had. Trust me I've been there. Not a soul knew (which was my first mistake trying to do it alone.) I had my husband kids and plenty others standing behind me. I am 31-year-old and I'm still going through sickness, but I promise you with God. I also started using what I'm going through to be a testimony to others. I used it to show he's still in the blessing business.

I would like for the person reading this to find courage, strength, and power through God as well as this book. Know that you're never alone. My prayer for you is that God gives you strength where none can be found. Power where you feel powerless and courage of the mightiest lion. I pray this and so much more.

Be strong in any situation if its grief, loss of job, or just plain weary. You must push through the battle to win the war!

Jessica Shelton

In Honor of BLM

Dear black people,

I'm sorry that they see u as a threat

the way u walk and talk

they see u as a threat

the color of your skin

they see u as a threat

you go to school to further your education

they see you as a threat

you get a nice house, nice car, you speak with much intellect

they see you as a threat

your pants pulled up your shirt tucked in

they see u as a threat

you walk home with skittles & iced tea in your neighborhood u a suspect &

they see you as a threat

you go to the store with a 20$ bill that is said to be fake, u have no gun, no knife, no weapon to first they still see u as a threat

8 min 46 sec. Their knee sat on your neck you get pulled over & asked for license u reach to get it & u r shot cold because

they saw u as a threat

as you slept in your bed you were shot 8 times, I wonder blk queen did they see u as a threat

I'm sorry blk ppl that they see you as a threat

all bc of the color of ur skin

one day our skin will fit in

& maybe we won't be a threat

but I love your melanin skin & how it glistens in the sun like an unopened honey bun

but just be strong my black ppl change is soon to come

Jessica Shelton

Marco Loud- Peter Gaines- Torrey Robinson- Darius Robinson- Kevin Hicks- Mary Truxillo- Demarcus Semer- Willie Tillman- Terril Thomas- Sylville Smith- Alton Sterling- Philando Castile- Terence Crutcher- Paul O'Neal- Alteria Woods- Bobby Russ- Jordan Edwards- Aaron Baily- Ronell Foster- Stephon Clark- Antwon Rose II- Botham Jean- Pamela Turner- Dominique Clayton- Atatiana Jefferson- Christopher Whitfield- Christopher McCorvey- Eric Reason- Korryn Gaines- Rekia Boyd- Kionte Spencer- Darius Tarver- Kobe Dimock- Heisler- Corey Jones- Tyre King- Michael Lorenzo Dean- Trayvon Martin- Renisha McBride- Oscar Grant III- Breonna Taylor- Kalief Browder- William Green- Ahmaud Arbery- Tony McDade- George Floyd

www.ingramcontent.com/pod-product-compliance
Lightning Source LLC
Chambersburg PA
CBHW052123110526
44592CB00013B/1727

speak out in relation to a major theological controversy, in which the Church's clear and unchangeable teaching was being challenged by powerful voices inside as well as outside the Church. Furthermore, this failure was deliberate and calculated. Ross Williamson was not engaging in febrile conspiracy-theorising when he attributed it to ecumenical concerns: these were certainly part of the explanation. The architect of the liturgical reforms, Father, later Archbishop, Annibale Bugnini, writing of the revision of the Good Friday Intercessions in *L'Osservatore Romano* in 1965, noted his motivation:

> And yet it is the love of souls and the desire to help in any way the road to union of the separated brethren, by removing every stone that could even remotely constitute an obstacle or difficulty, that has driven the Church to make even these painful sacrifices.[1]

On the specific issues Ross Williamson focuses on, the Lutheran denial of transubstantiation and of the sacrificial nature of the Mass, the silence of the new texts has been of continuing significance. In 2001, Cardinal Joseph Ratzinger (later Pope Benedict XVI) said, in a lecture:

> A sizable party of catholic liturgists seems to have practically arrived at the conclusion that Luther, rather than Trent, was substantially

---

1 *L'Osservatore Romano*, March 19, 1965

right in the sixteenth century debate; one can detect much the same position in the post conciliar discussions on the Priesthood.... It is only against this background of the effective denial of the authority of Trent, that the bitterness of the struggle against allowing the celebration of Mass according to the 1962 Missal, after the liturgical reform, can be understood. The possibility of so celebrating constitutes the strongest, and thus (for them) the most intolerable contradiction of the opinion of those who believe that the faith in the Eucharist formulated by Trent has lost its value.[2]

In short, Ross Williamson was right to draw attention to this point: the failure of this text to affirm what so many were denying, and which for that very reason needed to be affirmed more clearly than ever. He was right, again, to draw attention (as Michael Davies also did in his 1976 book *Cranmer's Godly Order*) to the way that the faith of the people was subverted in the 16th century in the context of a liturgy which was for the most part simply *silent* about those points its authors wished to deny, including the Real Presence and the sacrificial nature of the Mass.

---

[2] "The Theology of the Liturgy" in Alcuin Reid (ed.) *Looking Again at the Question of the Liturgy with Cardinal Ratzinger: Proceedings of the July 2001 Fontgombault Liturgical Conference* (Farnborough: St Michael's Abbey Press, 2003) pp. 18–33, p. 20.

Foreword

These points are distinct, nevertheless, from the question of sacramental validity. It is surely not necessary for the validity of a sacramental formula that it excludes all possible interpretations contrary to the teaching of the Church, however urgent it may be to oppose particular errors. Indeed, given the protean nature of heresy, such a requirement could conflict with the stability of the liturgy over time.

However convenient it may be to certain theologians wishing to deny particular truths about which key liturgical texts are silent — particularly when these texts were brought in to replace others which were *not* silent — it is also the case that it cannot be said that the Church as a whole has ceased to oppose the errors in question, even in the context of the reformed liturgy. The *Novus Ordo Missæ* still contains the Roman Canon, as Eucharistic Prayer I: this Missal, considered as a whole, is incompatible with a denial of these truths for this reason alone.

It remains true that Transubstantiation and the nature of the Mass as a sacrifice have been played down, and in practice even more than in theory, since Eucharistic Prayer I is not often used. They are among many teachings of the Church in which preaching and catechesis are needed to supplement the reformed liturgy.

This is not my opinion, I hasten to say, but that of the Holy See. Surprising as it may seem, it is something of a theme in post-Conciliar documents on the liturgy that innovations which are permitted may be theologically misleading. The reception of Holy Communion in the hand does not contradict, but it could cast doubt on the Real Presence: what can be done? Catechesis!

> The result of this catechesis should be to remove any suggestion of wavering on the part of the Church in its faith in the eucharistic presence, and also to remove any danger or even suggestion of profanation.[3]

Reception of Holy Communion under Both Kinds, similarly, might suggest the heresy of Utraquism: that one needs to receive both. So it must be

> preceded and continually accompanied by proper catechesis regarding the dogmatic principles on this matter laid down by the Ecumenical Council of Trent.[4]

The service of the altar by females, again, may undermine belief in the necessity of the all-male priesthood. To counter this:

> it would remain important to explain clearly to the faithful the nature of this innovation,

---

[3] Congregation for Divine Worship (1969) Instruction *Memoriale Domini*

[4] Congregation for Divine Worship (2004) Instruction *Redemptionis Sacramentum* 100

Foreword

lest confusion might be introduced, thereby hampering the development of priestly vocations.[5]

This is to speak only of liturgical changes authorised by the proper authorities. The liturgy one actually experiences in the context of the *Novus Ordo* is all too often marred by abuses. As Pope John Paul II noted in 2003:

> In various parts of the Church abuses have occurred, leading to confusion with regard to sound faith and Catholic doctrine concerning this wonderful sacrament. At times one encounters an extremely reductive understanding of the Eucharistic mystery. Stripped of its sacrificial meaning, it is celebrated as if it were simply a fraternal banquet.[6]

Not only has orthodox catechesis not always shored up the doctrines that are no longer made clear by the reformed texts and ceremonies, but many priests have taken the disappearance of the clear liturgical expression of the Faith in certain respects as justification for taking the matter even further, by supressing other aspects of the liturgy which conflict with their pet heresies. This had already started happening, indeed, in the period

---

[5] Letter dated July 27, 2001; published in *Notitiæ* 421–422 Vol 37 (2001) Num 8–9, pp. 397–399, at p. 399
[6] Pope John Paul II Encyclical Letter (2003) *Ecclesia de Eucharistia* 10

of "experimentation" preceding the publication of the *Novus Ordo Missæ*.

Hugh Ross Williamson deserves our gratitude for expressing the fundamental problem: that of a liturgy which, while it does not deny them, nevertheless seems *embarrassed* by the very teachings which express its inner nature. Jacques Maritain expressed a similar idea in 1967, when he wrote despairingly that "Christians are on their knees before the world".[7]

For the Church to get up off her knees, and to renew her task of evangelisation, she must as an institution shake off her embarrassment about the ancient Mass, and accord it a place of honour in her liturgical life.

Joseph Shaw
Senior Research Fellow,
St Benet's Hall, Oxford University,
Chairman of the Latin Mass Society

---

7 Jacques Maritain (1967) *The Peasant of the Garonne: An Old Layman Questions Himself about the Present Time,* p. 61

INTRODUCTION

Hugh Ross Williamson was born in 1901 and began his life as the son of a Minister in the Congregational Non-Conformist Church, one of the many off-shoots of the Protestant Church. From this religious position Hugh Ross Williamson moved towards Anglicanism in adulthood and in 1943 became an Anglo-Catholic priest, earning a substantial reputation for his sermons, preaching in many churches including St. Paul's Cathedral and Westminster Abbey. Finally, in 1955, he converted to Roman Catholicism, became a layman and concentrated on his historical writing.

Before becoming a priest he had been a writer, pursuing a path in journalism as an editor, then as a playwright, a broadcaster, but above all as an historian, specialising in Reformation History. His focus was to challenge the Protestant bias and uncover the truth which had been obscured by Protestant historians, generally known as "The Whig Interpretation of History." This version had not yet been seriously challenged, and those who dared, like Hugh Ross Williamson, received the scorn of academics.

Hugh Ross Williamson wrote many books contesting this accepted view, the most famous of which was

The Gunpowder Plot, written in 1951, and to which a simpler version was added in 1964 called *Guy Fawkes*. These showed how the Plot was suggested, (unbeknown to the admittedly hot-headed team) by Sir Robert Cecil, Secretary of State, via Lord Monteagle, one of the plotters' cousins. The "discovery" of this Plot led to the criminalising of Catholics and their religion for a further 220 years.

The Beginning of the English Reformation (1957) and *The Day Shakespeare Died* (1962) were a further two books which questioned the Protestant version of history; the latter explored the probability that Shakespeare was a Catholic, which shocked many readers in 1962 but it is a view now almost accepted because of more recent publications on this subject.

Another branch of his life was writing plays for the theatre as well as broadcasts for BBC Radio. He had a regular and popular programme in the 1950's on which he aired his short historical essays called "Enigmas of History" and "Historical Whodunnits." In 1958 Ross Williamson's "Mime of Bernadette" was performed at The Albert Hall, London and his book, *The Challenge of Bernadette* came out in the same year. One of his most successful plays, "Teresa of Avila" (1961) began at the Edinburgh Festival, then en route to London transferred to the Liverpool Playhouse where at one of the performances, the auditorium, which seated over

Introduction

seven hundred, was filled entirely by nuns and priests. From there it went to London's West End, the role of St. Teresa played by the famous Dame Sybil Thorndike. All these took place in the heady days before Vatican II.

More importantly, in 1955, just as he was about to leave the Anglican Church and submit to Rome, he wrote *The Great Prayer*. This book, in which each prayer of the Roman Canon of the Mass is examined both theologically and devotionally, has been well-read by priests, and is now reprinted by Gracewing. These prayers, unchanged, are those said by St. Augustine the first time he celebrated Mass in Canterbury in 597 AD. As the faith of Christians of all denominations in England (and the further English-speaking world) comes from St. Augustine's arrival, there should be nothing in these prayers with which to disagree. The author believed that by understanding this, later controversies could be resolved and the cause of Christian Unity advanced.

How wrong he was! Instead, at Vatican II, the Catholic Church sidelined the Roman Canon, introduced the options of Canons 2, 3 and 4, and removed the Offertory prayers, replacing them with others which made light of preparing to offer a Sacrifice. The aim of these changes was to achieve unity by the methods of Luther and Cranmer rather than of Saint Augustine.

Because of his religious journey from Non-Conformism to Anglicanism and thence to Catholicism, together with a detailed historical knowledge of the Reformation, Hugh Ross Williamson was in a pre-eminent position to understand what was actually taking place in the changes to the Mass. His main concern was that with the emphasis on the Sacrifice of Our Lord removed, the Mass was transformed into a memorial meal that could be said by any of the Christian denominations. He was one of the very first laymen to raise these concerns which were outlined in two pamphlets: *The Modern Mass: A Reversion to the Reforms of Cranmer* (1969) and *The Great Betrayal* (1970) which are being republished in one volume for the first time by Arouca Press.

Some readers may be uneasy to discover that Hugh Ross Williamson concluded that using Canon Two would render the Mass invalid as it could be said by any Protestant pastor without infringing his beliefs and was intended for this purpose. He therefore felt that as the *intentions* of those creating this Mass were to exclude or play down the sacrificial element as well as Christ's transubstantiation in order to replace it with a supper and a symbolic presence of Christ, how was this any different from the Reformation changes made by Cranmer?

Therefore, by association, Canons 3 and 4 would be invalid as written by the same team. Obviously that is his view and one not shared by many, but it is of interest.

Introduction

The other point he made to support the invalidity was the mistranslation of the words of Jesus in the consecration of the wine into His blood. In the Latin they were the same but in the English translation the words "shed for you and for many" became "shed for you and for all". This has now been corrected in recent translations because of much criticism, so is no longer relevant to this argument.

Hugh Ross Williamson was amongst the founding members of The Latin Mass Society (1964) and its first Vice-Chairman. This Society managed to persuade the Archbishop of Westminster, John Cardinal Heenan, to ask Pope Paul VI for an Indult allowing for the Tridentine Mass to be said in England.

This was granted insofar as it was "limited to certain groups on special occasions . . . provided that such groups make the request for reasons of genuine devotion." It was a small start, that would be followed by the Indult of Pope John Paul II in 1984 and finally by Pope Benedict XVI's *Summorum Pontificum* in 2007, which has allowed the Mass of Ages to be said legitimately once more. Such was the situation until 16th July 2021, when Pope Francis issued his own motu proprio, *Traditionis Custodes* (a curious title considering it proposes the demolition of the Traditional Liturgy). This overturns Pope Benedict XVI's generous *Summorum Pontificum* and the attack on the Traditional Latin Mass is once more renewed.

Sadly he did not live to see these later developments, as he died in January 1978, but at his Requiem Mass he had a splendid send-off in the Tridentine Rite, which the then Cardinal of Westminster, Basil Hume, tried to forbid. This was resolved by the Cardinal sending one of his priests from the Cathedral, Father Michael Ware, to say it.

Hugh Ross Williamson and his wife Margaret, my parents, are buried in St Mary's Cemetery, Kensal Green, London and on their headstone are the lines from a G. K. Chesterton poem, "To Paradise by way of Kensal Green."

Addendum: A paragraph from a longer letter to Hugh Ross Williamson from Mary G C Neilson, the Honourable Secretary of Una Voce, Scottish Branch. Dated 04/07/1970.

> Dear Mr. Ross Williamson,
>
> First of all let me congratulate you on your booklet "The Great Betrayal", which is even better than "The Modern Mass" as it has a wider appeal because it does not deal so exclusively with English history. There are one or two very valuable points in it which I am using in the course of arguments with various people: for example the confusion over the Ecumenical Movement and the Ecumenical Councils; also regarding the Lutheran

Introduction

professor from Gottingen whose advice was asked about the New Mass. I now have 100 copies of your book in this house and am busy distributing them throughout the world."

Julia Ashenden
August 6, 2021
Feast of the Transfiguration

PART I
The Modern Mass

A REVERSION TO THE REFORMS OF CRANMER (1969)

> "The fort is betrayed even of them that should have defended it."
> — St. John Fisher to his apostate colleagues

> "A weak clergy, lacking grace constantly to stand to their learning."
> — St. Thomas More to his daughter.

I

Cranmer's Objective

AN ENGLISH HISTORIAN IS APT, by the nature of things, to be suspicious of liturgical change. He knows that in his country it has happened before and that the consequences of it have molded his religious background. What he does not always realize is that few but specialists are interested in so circumscribed a subject and that the general condonation—so it seems—of certain actions springs not from bad faith but from ignorance.

It is my purpose here to set down quite simply the method by which the Faith was destroyed in England by measures for which the main responsibility rests on Thomas Cranmer, Archbishop of Canterbury, who was all-powerful in the religious sphere from 1547 to 1553.

He was honest enough about his intentions and made no effort to hide his opinion that the power of "the great harlot, that is to say, the pestiferous see of Rome" lay in "the popish doctrine of transubstantiation, of the real presence of Christ's flesh and blood in the sacrament of the altar (as they call it) and of the sacrifice and oblation of Christ made by the priest for the salvation of the quick and the dead."[1] It was

---
1 Cranmer: *Defence*, 1

this that must be destroyed. People must learn that Christ was not in the Sacrament but only in the worthy receivers of the Sacrament. "The eating and drinking of Christ's flesh and blood is not to be taken in the common signification, with mouth and teeth to eat a thing being present, but by a lively faith, in heart and mind to digest a thing being absent."[2] The new rite which Cranmer devised to embody this belief, "the administration of the Holy Supper," must have nothing in it which could be "twisted" to resemble "the never-sufficiently-to-be-execrated Mass." And that in the Mass "there is offered to God the Father a sacrifice, namely the body and blood of our Lord, truly and really, in order to obtain the forgiveness of sins and to obtain the salvation as well of the dead as of the living"[3] was defined as a heresy deserving the death-penalty.

So much for Cranmer's objective. The three chief means by which he attained it were: 1) the use of the vernacular; 2) the substitution of a Holy Table for an altar and 3) changes made in the Canon of the Mass.

---

2 *Ibid*, III
3 *Reformatio*

II

The Vernacular

THE TRANSLATION OF THE BIBLE into the vernacular had existed in England since Saxon days. Long before Wyclif had made his "translation" in 1380, there had been, as St. Thomas More pointed out, English translations "by virtuous and learned men" and "by good and goodly people" before Wyclif "took it upon him of a malicious purpose to translate it anew." And More was insistent that there was no reason "why it was not convenient to have the Bible translated into the English tongue," for "there is no treatise of Scripture so hard but that a good virtuous man, or woman either, shall somewhat find therein that shall delight and increase their devotion." What was to be resisted was the deliberate mistranslation of the Bible "of malicious purpose" and it is this that provides the key for the insistent anti-Catholic demands for the vernacular in the sixteenth century.[1]

The translation made by William Tyndale, one of Cranmer's associates, was burnt by the Catholic

---

[1] *The English Hexapla*, published in 1805, contains six vernacular versions (of 1380, 1534, 1539, 1557, 1582 and 1611), printed in parallel columns. They include Wyclif's, Tyndale's and Cranmer's, and are invaluable for comparison.

authorities. When St. Thomas More was asked about it, he replied: "It is to me a great marvel that any good Christian man, having any drop of wit in his head, would anything marvel or complain of the burning of that book, if he knew the matter. Which whoso calleth the New Testament calleth it by a wrong name except they call it Tyndale's Testament or Luther's Testament. For so had Tyndale, after Luther's counsel, corrupted and changed it from the good and wholesome doctrine of Christ to the devilish heresies of their own, that it was a clean contrary thing." Asked for examples, he chose three words. "One is the word Priests. The other the Church. The third Charity. For Priests he always calls seniors; the Church he calleth always the congregation, and Charity he calleth love. Now do these names in our English tongue neither express the things that be meant by them, and there also appeareth, circumstances well considered, that he had a mischievous mind in the change."[2]

Tyndale also provided his translation with notes, such as that the Mass was a matter of "nodding, becking, mewing, as it were, apes play." Those who still believed the traditional faith and practice were "beasts without the seal of the Spirit of God, but sealed with the Mark of the Beast and cankered consciences."

---

[2] More's controversy with Tyndale includes the *Dialogue concerning Heresies* (1529) — from which this passage is taken — and the *Confutation of Tyndale's answer* (1532 and 1533).

The Vernacular

But far more damaging than the comments were, as More had pointed out, the deliberate mistranslations which Tyndale (and Cranmer, following him, in a version issued six years later) made in order to eradicate traditional Catholic doctrine. The word meaning "idols" he rendered by "images" and thereby forged a useful tool against the cultus of the Saints and the Sacred Humanity of Christ. "Confess," which might suggest the sacrament of penance, became "acknowledge." The great key-words of the Gospel, "grace" and "salvation," became "favor" and "health." The word which should have been "priest" he rendered as "elder" and "church" as "congregation" and noted: "By a priest, then, in the New Testament understand nothing but an elder to teach the younger." He also explained that the two sacraments which Christ ordained, Baptism and Holy Communion, were nothing but the preaching of Christ's promises." So, to take one example, in the Epistle of St. James, the apostolic advice: "Is any man sick among you? Let him bring in the priests of the Church, and let them pray over him anointing him with oil in the name of the Lord," with its obvious reference to the sacrament of Unction, could not be allowed to stand. Even Wyclif in his earlier translation had not tampered with this and had correctly translated "priests of the church." But in Tyndale's version and Cranmer's version they became "elders of the congregation."

The Protestants could thus appeal to the Bible in the vulgar tongue to bear witness that the New Testament contained no references to justify contemporary Catholic teaching on and practice of the doctrines in dispute; and when such tendentious mistranslations of the Bible were, quite properly, seized and suppressed by Catholic authorities, Catholics could be additionally accused of "trying to prevent the people from reading the Bible." It was as simple as that. And the effectiveness of the double lie was so complete that its echoes still reverberate.

At the very core of a vernacular Mass lay the vernacular account of the institution of the Eucharist. It was not only that the silent Canon, which had been the rule from the eighth century, must be abandoned, but that the English "Do this in remembrance of Me" should be "distinctly" heard.

The Greek word, *anamnesis*, which is translated as "in remembrance of," is difficult to render accurately in English. Words like "remembrance," "memory," and "memorial" imply the existence of something itself absent, whereas anamnesis has the sense of recalling or re-presenting a past event so that it becomes actively present. This meaning is not adequately caught even by the Latin *memoria*. The English words "recall" and "represent," even when written "re-call" and "re-present," are insufficient without further explanation; and "remembrance,"

The Vernacular

"memory" and "memorial," because of their conventional usage and common meaning, are actually misleading.

"The understanding of the Eucharist as 'for the *anamnesis* of Me' — as the 're-calling' before God of the one sacrifice of Christ in all its accomplished and effectual fullness so that it is here and now operative by its effects — is," as one theologian has put it, "clearly brought out in all traditions" of the early church. In the words of St. John Chrysostom: "We offer even now that which was then offered, which cannot be exhausted. This is done for an anamnesis of that which was then done, for 'Do this' said He, 'for the anamnesis of me.' We do not offer a different sacrifice like the high-priest of old, but we ever offer the same. Or rather we offer the *anamnesis* of the Sacrifice."[3]

Cranmer, who wished to root out any idea of the Mass as a sacrifice and to substitute the theory of a mere memorial meal in which Christ was not present except in the hearts of the worshippers, could not have found a more potent weapon than the abandonment of the silent Canon in favor of the Institution-narrative in English, with its reiterated "Do this in remembrance of me." In the great silence, the ordinary worshipper, instructed in the meaning of the Moment, knew, even if he could not formulate it, what was happening. But

---

[3] Gregory Dix, *The Shape of the Liturgy*, p. 243 (1944) quoting St. John Chrysostom in *Heb. Hom* xvii. 3

now he could hear for himself that, as far as he could understand it, it *was* a memorial meal. The Bible said so. He was called upon to remember something that had happened long ago in the past. And this interpretation was emphasized by the words spoken by the minister giving him his communion: "Take and eat this in remembrance that Christ died for thee and feed on him in thy heart by faith, with thanksgiving."

The imposition of the new vernacular Prayer Book on the country took place on Whitsunday, 9th June 1549. On June 10th, a body of Devonshire peasants, having sampled the new service, forced their parish priest to restore the Mass. Within ten days a people's army, possibly six thousand strong — the figures are difficult to arrive at — had taken Crediton and were menacing Exeter. Their demands were simple and pointed and concerned solely with the Faith. They asked that the Mass should be restored "as before" and that the Blessed Sacrament should be again reserved in a prominent position. "We will not," they said, "receive the new service because it is but like a Christmas game, but we will have our old service of Mattins, Mass, Evensong and Procession (the Litany of Our Lady) in Latin and we will have every preacher in his sermon and every priest at his Mass pray by name for the souls in Purgatory as our forefathers did." Baptism should be available "as well on week-days as on holy-days." The Blessings of simple things should

The Vernacular

be restored, palms and ashes should be distributed at the accustomed times with "all the ancient old ceremonies used heretofore by our Mother, the Holy Church" (which Cranmer had abolished as "superstitions").[4]

Cranmer was incensed not only by the demands themselves but, even more, by the fact that ignorant peasants, "Hob, Will and Dick," should presume to question his theology. He wrote to them: "Oh, ignorant men of Devonshire and Cornwall, as soon as ever I heard your articles I thought you were deceived by some crafty papists to make you ask you wist not what. You declare what spirit leadeth them that persuaded you that the Word of God is but like a Christmas game. It is more like a game and a foolish play to hear the priest speak aloud to the people in Latin. In the English service there is nothing but the eternal Word of God. If it be to you but a Christmas game, I think you not so much to be blamed as the papistical priests who have abused your sincerity. Had you rather be like pies or parrots that be taught to speak and yet not understand one word of what they say than be true Christians who pray to God in faith?"[5]

---

[4] The Fifteen Articles of the rebels are printed in Strype's *Cranmer*, Appendix XI; there are other versions, though the demands here quoted are common to all, and the whole matter is chronicled in F. Rose-Troup, *The Western Rebellion* of 1549.
[5] The very long and bitter letter from which this extract is taken is printed in full in Jenkyns, *Remains of Thomas Cranmer*, Vol. II and there is a short, six-page abstract in Mason's *Cranmer*.

THE MODERN MASS

The rebels, in their simple faith, paid no heed to the learned Archbishop. Cranmer had to rely on the secular arm. Foreign mercenaries, mainly German Lutherans, were employed on English soil for the first time for three hundred years and the last stand for the Faith was defeated in battle. "The killing was indiscriminate," in Hilaire Belloc's memorable words: "four thousand were shot down or ridden down or hanged before the men of Devon would accept, without enthusiasm, the exquisite prose of Cranmer."[6] Of the Italian and Spanish adventurers, who reinforced the Germans, it is recorded that, when they realized what had been at stake, they went to the Imperial Nuncio to be absolved for what they done.

When the news of the vernacular victory reached London, Cranmer "made a collation in Paul's choir for the victory" and in a sermon before the Lord Mayor and Aldermen the Archbishop admonished his auditors that "the plague of division among ourselves, the like of which has not been heard of since the Passion of Christ, is come upon us by the instigation of the Devil, in that we have not been diligent hearers of God's Word by His true preachers but have been led away by Popish priests."

It was, of course, quite untrue that the people did not understand the Latin Mass. The circulation of devotional and instructional books among the population

---

6 A History of England, vol. iv.

The Vernacular

of three million may be gauged by the fact that, in the holocaust of Catholic learning and piety which was part of the Protestant policy, a quarter of a million of liturgical books alone were destroyed. The year after the enforcement of the first Prayer Book — 1550 — Cranmer sent commissioners to the universities. In Oxford, thousands of books were destroyed. Cambridge suffered a slower but even more drastic denudation, which ensured that there were, at the beginning of Queen Elizabeth's reign, no more than 177 "cut and mangled" volumes left.

The result was inevitable. A Protestant preacher, in a sermon before the King in 1552, did not scruple to point out: "There is entering into England more blind ignorance, superstition and infidelity than ever was under Romish bishops. Your realm (which I am sorry to speak) shall become more barbarous than Scythia."[7] Another, deploring the multiplicity of sects which were the inevitable concomitant of Cranmer's policy, complained: "There are Arians, Marcionites, Libertines, Davists and the like monstrosities in great numbers; we have need of help against the sectaries and Epicureans and pseudo-evangelicals who are beginning to shake our churches with greater violence than ever."[8]

---

7 Sermon by Bernard Gilpin, quoted in F. O. W. Hawel's *Sketches of the Reformation taken from the Contemporary Pulpit*.
8 *Original Letters relative to the English Reformation*, vol. ii, Micronius to Bullinger (May 1550).

One reason for the mangling of the books was the Act which Cranmer drew up because "it has been noised and bruited abroad that they should have again their old Latin service" and it was necessary to see that the people "put away all such vain expectation of having the public service and the administration of the Sacraments again in the Latin tongue." The Act ordered the surrender of all Latin service books for the authorities to "so deface and abolish them that they never after may serve any such use as they were provided for." There was one exception. Copies in Latin or English of the Primer of Henry VIII were allowed, provided that all mention of the saints was erased.

For Cranmer hated the saints almost as much as he hated the Mass, and one of the advantages of the vernacular was that he could issue a new litany, from which all the names of the saints were omitted — as well as that of Our Lady — and the petition inserted "From the tyranny of the Bishop of Rome and all his detestable enormities, good Lord deliver us," which could be easily "understood of the people" when it was said every Wednesday and Friday.

III
The Holy Table

WITHIN A YEAR OF CRANMER'S accession to full ecclesiastical power, one of the foreign Protestants in England wrote exultantly to Bullinger, who had succeeded Zwingli in Zurich: "*Aræ facta sunt haræ*"—the altars have been made into pigsties.[1] It was not at that point quite true, for in various places altars were retained by pious priests and congregations. But in November of 1550, Cranmer, through the Privy Council, issued an edict that all altars throughout the kingdom should be destroyed. For the future, wherever the rite for the Holy Eucharist was celebrated, a wooden table was to be used.

With the order was sent Cranmer's explanation, which, as Philip Hughes in his definitive work on *The Reformation in England* (p. 121) has said "leaves no doubt that one religion was being substituted for another." The "certain considerations"[2] pointed out: "The form of a table shall move the simple from the superstitious opinion of the Popish Mass unto the

---

[1] John ab Ulmis to Bullinger, in *Original Letters* II
[2] *Reasons why the Lord's Board should rather be after the form of a Table than of an Altar*: printed in full in Parker Society Cranmer II.

right use of the Lord's Supper. For the use of an altar is to make sacrifice upon it: the use of a table is to serve men to eat upon. If we come to feed upon Him, spiritually to eat his body and spiritually to drink his blood, which is the true use of the Lord's Supper, then no man can deny that the form of a table is more meet for the Lord's board than the form of an altar."

Cranmer went on to explain that, where he had retained the word "altar" in his new Prayer Book, it meant "the table where Holy Communion is distributed" and that it then could be called an altar because there was offered there "*our* sacrifice of praise and thanksgiving."

The edict was enforced rigidly. When one of the bishops[3] declined to remove the altars in his diocese, he was imprisoned and deprived of his see. In London, the alterations were immediate and sweeping. The bishop, who had been one of Cranmer's chaplains, determined to make the new table as far as possible inaccessible to non-communicants. A contemporary chronicle[4] records that, in St. Paul's Cathedral, "he removed the table into the middle of the upper choir and set the ends east and west and after the Creed caused a veil to be drawn that no person should see but those that received; and he closed the iron gratings of the choir

---

3   George Day of Chichester.
4   Wriothesley's.

The Holy Table

on the north and south side with brick and plaster, that none might remain in at the choir."

Since there was no Real Presence and no Sacrifice, it was logical enough to attempt to get rid of non-communicating attendance at the Eucharist and Cranmer laid down that "there shall be no celebration of the Lord's Supper, except there be a good number to communicate with the priest at his discretion; and if there be not above twenty persons in the parish of discretion, there shall be no Communion, except four, or three at the least, communicate with the priest. And to take away the superstition which any person hath, or might have, in the bread and wine, it shall suffice that the bread be such as is usual to be eaten at table with other meats, but the best and purest wheat bread that conveniently may be gotten. And if any of the bread and wine remain, the curate shall have it to his own use."[5]

"The last stone to be piled on the cairn below which lay the ancient belief in the Holy Eucharist" — the phrase is Philip Hughes's — was the attack on kneeling to receive communion. What was this but idolatry? A rubric was rapidly inserted in the new Prayer Book explaining that "it is not meant thereby that any adoration is done or ought to be done either unto the sacramental bread or wine there bodily received or to

---

[5] Rubrics at end of 1552 Prayer Book Communion Service.

THE MODERN MASS

any real or essential presence there being of Christ's natural flesh and blood."[6]

The table, as time went on, became more of a table and was moved about for utilitarian purposes. Explicit instructions were issued that "the holy table in every church is to be set in the place where the altar stood, saving when the communion of the sacrament is to be distributed; at which time the same shall be so placed in good sort within the chancel, as whereby the minister may be more conveniently heard of the communicants in his prayer and ministration and the communicants also more conveniently and in more number communicate with the said minister. And after the communion done the same holy table is to be placed where it stood before."

It was left to the Puritans in the following century to carry Cranmer's work to its logical conclusion and not only to receive communion sitting but to use the table as a convenient place on which to put their hats.

---

6 The so-called "Black Rubric" in the 1552 Prayer Book.

IV

The Canon of the Mass

THE VERNACULAR AND THE HOLY Table were the practical means by which Cranmer accustomed the ordinary people of England to the new doctrines. They could now, by their corporate action, understand that a simple meal was not a Sacrifice—the Sacrifice—and that it involved eating nothing but ordinary bread and wine; and they could hear that it was merely in memory of something done long ago. It was because such usage was more potent for the theologically unlearned than any doctrinal teaching that, in the short five-year reign of Mary the Catholic, when England returned for the last time to the Faith, Cardinal Pole insisted on restoring not only the altars and the Mass but simple ceremonies which Cranmer had abolished—holy water, ashes and palms—"in the observation of which beginneth the very education of the children of God" and the abolition of which the heretics "make a first point" in their attempt to destroy the Church."[1]

But the core of Cranmer's work, of course, was the theological statement of the new beliefs in liturgical

---

[1] Pole's great sermon on St. Andrew's Day, is admirably summarised in Philip Hughes: *The Reformation in England*, vol. 2 pp. 246-253.

form. His final version of what had once been the Mass was, as Gregory Dix has insisted, "*not* a disordered attempt at a Catholic rite, but the only effective attempt ever made to give liturgical expression to the doctrine of 'justification by faith alone.'"[2] And, thus considered, it is a masterpiece.

The logical consequences of the basic Protestant doctrine of "faith alone" were — and are — the abolition of the sacraments. External actions obviously cannot be accepted as causes in the realm of grace. Luther, of course, had seen this from the beginning and had abolished the five "lesser" sacraments at the same time as he had attacked communion in one kind, transubstantiation, and the doctrine of the Eucharist as a sacrifice, as the first stages of devaluing what — since both baptism and holy communion are indubitably commanded in the New Testament — he could not deny. As it was impossible to rid Christianity of these external acts of baptism and the Eucharist, it was essential to empty them of any intelligible meaning. On this all the Protestant sects were at one, the Zwinglians and the Calvinists no less than the Lutherans.

Cranmer agreed, as he was bound to, with Zwingli's logic that "the doctrine, *Sola fides justificat*, is a foundation and principle to deny the presence of Christ's body

---

[2] Dix: *The Shape of the Liturgy*, p. 672.

The Canon of the Mass

really in the Sacrament"³ and, as we have seen, he therefore attacked the Mass as vehemently as had Luther in his famous: "I declare that all the brothels (though God has reproved them severely), all manslaughters, murders, thefts and adulteries have wrought less evil than the abomination of the popish mass."⁴

Cranmer's alternative to the Mass is included in the two Prayer Books of 1549 and 1552. Like later engineers of change, he thought it best to bring it about gradually so as not immediately to arouse opposition,⁵ but there is no doubt that the 1552 version was in his mind from the beginning; and as "1552 still supplies the whole structure of the present [Anglican] liturgy and some ninety five per cent of its wording"⁶ it is the 1552 rite alone that will be considered here.

The Canon was divided into three parts and became the "Prayer for the Church Militant," the "Prayer of Consecration" and the so-called "Prayer of Oblation."

---

3 Stephen Gardiner, the Catholic Bishop of Winchester, who was imprisoned by Cranmer for his defense of the Eucharist, quotes Zwingli's admission in the course of his controversy with Cranmer. See *The Letters of Stephen Gardiner*, p. 277.

4 *Werke* (ed. Weimar 1888) xv. P. 773.

5 cf. Cardinal Heenan's Pastoral Letter of October 12th, 1969. "'Why does the Mass keep changing?' Here is the answer. It would have been foolhardy to introduce all the changes at once. It was obviously wiser to change gradually and gently. If all the changes had been introduced together, you would have been shocked."

6 Dix: *op. cit.* p. 669.

Roughly speaking, the first of these corresponds to the *Te Igitur*, *Memento Domine*, and *Communicantes*: the second to *Hanc Igitur*, *Quam Oblationem* and *Qui Pridie*; and the third to *Unde et memores*, *Supra quæ* and *Supplices te rogamus*. (There is no parallel to the *Memento Etiam*, the *Nobis quoque peccatoribus* or the *Per Quem*). To see exactly what Cranmer did, these three sections must be considered in detail.

V

The Prayer for the Church Militant

THE "PRAYER FOR THE CHURCH Militant" runs: "Almighty and everliving God, which by the holy apostle has taught us to make prayers and supplications, and to give thanks for all men; we humbly beseech thee most mercifully to accept our alms and to receive these our prayers which we offer unto thy divine Majesty, beseeching thee to inspire continually the universal church with the spirit of truth, unity and concord. And grant that all they that do confess thy holy name may agree in the truth of thy holy Word and live in unity and godly love. We beseech thee also to save and defend all Christian Kings, Princes and Governors, and specially thy servant Edward our King, that under him we may be godly and quietly governed; and grant unto his whole council and to all that be put in authority under him that they may truly and indifferently administer justice, to the punishment of wickedness and vice and to the maintenance of God's true religion and virtue. Grant grace (O heavenly father) to all Bishops, Pastors and Curates that they may both by their life and doctrine set forth thy true and lively

Word and rightly and duly administer thy holy sacraments: and to all thy people give thy heavenly grace, and especially to this congregation here present, that with meek heart and due reverence they may hear and receive thy Holy Word, truly serving thee in holiness and righteousness all the days of their life. And We most humbly beseech thee of thy goodness (O Lord) to comfort and succor all them which in this transitory life be in trouble, sorrow, need, sickness or any other adversity. Grant this, O father, for Jesus Christ's sake, our only mediator and advocate. Amen."

The change is sufficiently dramatic. Apart from the omissions of the Pope and the saints, which were only to be expected, what has disappeared is any mention of the oblations *haec dona*, *haec munera*, *haec sancta sacrificia illibata* which are so essential a part of the *Te Igitur*.

In the ancient liturgy of the Church, great honor had always been paid to the offerings of the bread and the wine. They are the *immaculatam hostiam*, the *calicem salutaris* of the offertory prayers, as well as the assertion of excellence in the *Te Igitur*, to be presented to God, with the request to make them in *omnibus benedictam, adscriptam, ratam, rationabilem, acceptabilemque*, for the coming miracle of transubstantiation. And "always," as Jungmann has shown, "it is the thought of their imminent transubstantiation that has conditioned the

The Prayer for the Church Militant

insistence on their sanctity."[1] This alone was anathema to Cranmer. "Like Luther he believed that any form of offertory 'stank of oblation.'"[2] He therefore abolished all the offertory prayers, even what many might consider the most beautiful of them, *Deus, qui humanæ*, and all mention of the "oblation" of bread and wine.

Cranmer's difficulty was that the placing of the bread and wine upon the altar *looked* as far as the people were concerned, as the offertory always had. If the congregation was to be taught an entirely new idea, something more was required. This Cranmer found in arranging for the church-wardens at this point to make a collection of money and by referring only to "alms" in the prayer. As the alms had not been offered or even handled by the minister, there could be no danger of their being thought of as an "oblation" in the old sense. As an ingenious piece of liturgical workmanship, it does indeed, as Gregory Dix has said, deserve admiration.

And, of course, the reference to "alms" only was heard and understood by the congregation. For it was of the essence of the "reform" that the silent Canon, which had been in use since the eighth century,[3] was

---

1 Jungmann: *Missa Sollemnia*, iii. P. 62, n. 19.
2 Dix: *op. cit* p. 661.
3 It was ordered that "pontifex *tacite* intrat in canonem," though *à voix basse* was not necessarily interpreted everywhere as "*dune voix absolument imperceptibile*": Jungmann op. cit p. 9.

abolished so that the new vernacular should have its due effect on the people.

To the changes effected by omission, Cranmer added one important one by the inclusion of the name of the sovereign in place of the Pope.

Sixteen years previously King Henry VIII had ordered Bidding Prayers in the vernacular by which, in the form of carefully-phrased petitions, people's thoughts should be directed in correct political and theological channels. Pre-eminently men were to be made to realize that the King was the supreme head of the Church in England. The Pope, if mentioned at all, was to be mentioned with contumely. The Bidding Prayers were a useful device for commenting on various aspects of contemporary life, but the reason for their introduction and the essence of their utility was in their emphasis on the sovereign. Cranmer, though abolishing the actual prayers, kept and emphasized that point, by putting the prayer for the King and the State (of which the church is merely a part) in place of the *Te Igitur* prayer for the Pope and the Church.[4]

So the "Prayer for the Church Militant," with its omission of any reference to the oblations, of Our Lady

---

[4] It is interesting to notice that the recent inclusion of Bidding Prayers in the Mass can — at least in England — have the same effect. Thus the first petition may be a prayer for the Queen and the Royal Family which, by the place in the Mass, therefore take, in time, precedence of the Pope.

and the Saints, of the Pope and the world-wide Catholic Church and its inclusion of the Erastian head of State and Church, prepared the way for the consecration of the elements.

VI

The Prayer of Consecration

IN THE 1549 BOOK, CRANMER HAD prefaced the Words of Institution with: "Hear us, O merciful Father, We beseech thee; and with thy Holy Spirit and Word, vouchsafe to bless and sanctify these thy gifts and creatures of bread and wine that they may be unto us the body and blood of thy most dearly beloved son, Jesus Christ."

This formula was attacked on the grounds that it was capable of being construed as effecting transubstantiation. To this Cranmer replied indignantly: "We do not pray absolutely that the bread and Wine may be made the body and blood of Christ, but that *unto us* in that holy mystery they may be made so; that is to say, that we may so worthily receive the same that we may be partakers of Christ's body and blood, and that therefore in spirit and in truth we may be spiritually nourished."[1]

Yet though this formula expressed with exactitude the Zwinglian meaning of the rite — that is, the continual mental "remembering" of Christ's passion and death, which constitutes "eating the flesh and drinking the blood," and the offering of our souls and bodies to

---

1 Cranmer, Works, ed. Jenkyns III, 146, and Parker Society i. 79.

THE MODERN MASS

Christ, which constitutes the only "sacrifice" — Cranmer decided in the Second Book to remove any possibility of misunderstanding.

But before proceeding to this, it is necessary to make a digression into the present.

It is, of course, quite true that the word "nobis" exists in the *Quam Oblationem* of the Roman Canon — "be pleased to make this same offering wholly blessed, to consecrate it and approve it, making it reasonable and acceptable, so that it may become for us the Body and Blood." But here the sense is unequivocal, for the transubstantiation has been prepared for by the magnificent *Te Igitur*, *Memento Domine* and *Hanc Igitur* where the "holy, unblemished sacrificial gifts" are described in terms proper to the coming change into the Body and Blood, of which we are the unworthy beneficiaries. It is Cranmer's omission of these references to and elaborations on the oblations which justifies his defense of himself that his formula could not be confused with transubstantiation. It was merely "for us" in our minds, not objectively.

The alternative Canon, Anaphora II, now imposed on the Church, follows Cranmer with exactitude. For the consecration there is no preparation whatever. After the Benedictus, the celebrant merely says: "You are truly holy, Lord, the fount of all holiness" and then immediately prays that "these gifts may be made for

The Prayer of Consecration

us the Body and Blood." In the Roman Canon it is impossible to understand "nobis" in the Cranmerian sense; in Anaphora II it is almost impossible to understand it any other way. What makes it worse is that the instruction of the Consilium was that this Canon, Anaphora II, should be the one in ordinary use and, further, be utilized for catechetical instruction of the young in the nature of the Eucharistic Prayer.[2]

But to return to Cranmer and his removal of any possible misinterpretation or ambiguity in the prayer. In the 1552 version, it ran: "Hear us, O merciful Father, we beseech Thee; and grant that we, receiving these thy creatures of bread and wine, according to Thy Son, our Savior Jesus Christ's holy institution, in remembrance of his death and passion, may be partakers of his most blessed body and blood."

By the omission of "with Thy Holy Spirit and Word vouchsafe to bless and sanctify these Thy gifts and creatures of bread and wine that they may be unto us

---

[2] In July of 1968, knowing that many who knew Cranmer's work were seriously disturbed at the possibility of Anaphora II being phrased and used for the purpose of a spurious unity with Protestants for it can clearly be used to deny transubstantiation—I wrote in the *Catholic Herald* an appeal to the English Hierarchy (who know the whole story of Cranmer as well as I do) to ask the Consilium, as evidence of good faith, to delete the *nobis*. Nothing happened and one was forced to remember that the English Reformation was brought about by the apostasy of all the English bishops except one—St. John Fisher.

the body and blood of Thy most dearly beloved Son Jesus Christ," Cranmer destroys any implication that the gift of the Body and Blood is connected with the bread and wine and that "sanctify" betokens, in some sense, holiness.

The 1552 Prayer of Consecration begins "Almighty God, our heavenly father, which of thy tender mercy didst give thine only son Jesus Christ to suffer death upon the cross for our redemption, who made there (by his one oblation of himself once offered) a full, perfect and sufficient sacrifice, oblation and satisfaction for the sins of the whole world, and did institute and in his holy gospel command us to continue a perpetual memory of that his precious death until his coming again."

Here Gregory Dix has drawn attention to "the unmistakable emphasis on 'His one oblation of himself once offered, a full, perfect and sufficient sacrifice, oblation and satisfaction for the sins of the whole world,' long ago — on Calvary — and its relegation of the Eucharist to a 'perpetual *memory*' — a cleverly chosen word — 'of that His precious death until his coming again,' Where 'again' — not in St. Paul — emphasizes that as the Passion is in the past, so the 'coming' is in the future, not in the Eucharist."[3]

---

3 Dix: op. cit. p. 664.

VII
The Prayer of Oblation

THE PRAYER OF OBLATION, WHICH is said immediately after the Communion of the people, runs: "O Lord and heavenly Father, we thy humble servants entirely desire thy fatherly goodness mercifully to accept this our Sacrifice of praise and thanksgiving: most humbly beseeching thee to grant that by the merits and death of thy son, Jesus Christ, and through faith in his blood, we and all thy whole church may obtain remission of our sins and all other benefits of his passion. And here we offer and present unto thee, O Lord, ourselves, our souls and bodies to be a reasonable, holy and lively sacrifice unto thee; humbly beseeching thee that all we which be partakers of this holy Communion, may be fulfilled with thy grace and heavenly benediction. And although we be unworthy through our manifold sins to offer unto Thee any Sacrifice; yet we beseech thee to accept this our bounden duty and service, not weighing our merits but pardoning our offences, through Jesus Christ our Lord; by whom and with whom in the unity of the holy ghost, all honor and glory be unto thee, O father almighty, world without end. Amen."

Here, it will be noticed, Cranmer puts beyond doubt his new interpretation of the rite and by the three-fold use of the word "Sacrifice" confuses the issue for the simple who listen to the vernacular and are therefore ready to assume that the new Mass has some kind of continuity with the old.

The Catholic concept was that Christ offers His perfect oblation of Himself to the Father and that the earthly church as his Body enters into the eternal priestly act by the Eucharist. Cranmer deliberately substitutes for this the idea that we offer to God "*ourselves, our souls and bodies.*"

Again the "by whom and with whom in the unity of the holy ghost, all honor and glory be unto thee, O father almighty, world without end. Amen" is intended to give the impression of, but to be totally different from, the doxology — the greatest in liturgy — of the *Per Ipsum*: "*Per ipsum et cum ipso et in ipso, est tibi, Deo Patri omnipotenti, in unitate Spiritus Sancti, omnia honor et gloria, per omnia saecula saeculorum.*" Here, the five-fold sign of the Cross followed by the elevation of the Host and Chalice together in a gesture of offering (a remnant of the ancient ceremony in which the celebrant lifted up the consecrated Bread and the deacon the great two-handed Chalice and touched one with the other) was the outward and visible sign of the offering of the Acceptable Sacrifice to God. The actual elevation, coinciding with the words *omnis honor et gloria*, saw the symbolism of language and action fused

The Prayer of Oblation

into one and become a liturgical lesson in the meaning of the Mass.

Cranmer forbade the Crosses and the Elevation but kept an approximation to the words, which now meant something quite different, to give the illusion of continuity.

Thus the new rite was shaped to embody the belief in Justification by faith alone—a belief in which the sacraments, in the sense they had always been understood, could have no place.

VIII

The Question of Justification and the Tridentine Mass

IT WAS THE QUESTION OF JUSTIFI-cation which lay behind all the other matters with which the Council of Trent was called to deal—and it is too often forgotten that the Council was summoned to reconcile the differences between Catholic and Protestant but, after the most intensive debate lasting in all for eighteen years, recognized that those differences were unbridgeable. Between the Scriptural Catholic doctrine, based on James ii. 24, 26: "Do you see that by works a man is justified, and not by faith only? Faith without works is dead" and Luther's doctrine of the sole necessity of faith there could be no compromise.

At Trent the definition was promulgated in 1547: "If any man shall say that the wicked man is justified by faith alone, meaning that no other thing is required to co-operate for obtaining the grace of justification, and that it is not necessary for him to be prepared and disposed by the movement of his will, let him be anathema."

At the end of Trent, during which the Protestants everywhere made, like Cranmer, new rites embodying the heresy, "the great Catholic need had become that of unity and the closing of the ranks against the new negations. For this the old liturgy, in the same language everywhere, was too valuable an instrument to lose. The result was the reformed Roman Missal of Pius V, imposed on the whole Roman obedience by *an unprecedented legislative act of the central authority.* "[1]

This Tridentine Mass was enacted by St. Pius by his *Quo Primum* on July 19, 1570. He ruled that "by this our decree, to be valid in perpetuity, we determine and order that never shall anything be added to, omitted from or changed in this Missal." To bind posterity, he affirmed that "at no time in the future can a priest, whether secular or religious ever be forced to use any other way of saying Mass. And so as to preclude once for all any scruple of conscience and fear of ecclesiastical penalties and censures, we herewith declare that it is in virtue of our Apostolic Authority that we decree and determine that this our present order and decree is to last in perpetuity and can never be legally revoked or amended at a future date."

As this was delivered three centuries before the definition of Infallibility, it is perhaps pointless to argue

---

[1] Dix: op. cit. p. 619. I have quoted this from an Anglican source, because it emphasizes the point, which is a commonplace to theologians and historians, that Trent has a unique status and is not, as too many casual readers assume, just another Ecumenical Council. The italics are mine.

The Question of Justification and the Tridentine Mass

how far it is binding, though the "in virtue of our Apostolic Authority" suggests a reasonable rigidity. And certainly St. Pius's own estimation of its importance can be gauged from his "and if anyone would nevertheless dare to attempt any action contrary to this Order of ours, given for all times, let him know that he has incurred the wrath of Almighty God and of the Blessed Apostles Peter and Paul."

It is these prohibitions and censures of St. Pius which the present Pope has set aside in his Apostolic Constitution *Missale Romanum* of April 3, 1969, decreeing the new forms of Mass: "We wish these our decrees and prescriptions may be firm and effective now and in the future notwithstanding, to the extent necessary, the apostolic constitutions and ordinances issued by our predecessors."

The Tridentine Mass, forged as an everlasting weapon against heresy, is to be abandoned to a new form which is only too compatible with the heresies of Cranmer and his associates. Some of us wonder why.

London
The Feast of S. S. Peter and Paul,
July 12, 1969

SHORT BIBLIOGRAPHY

For the general history of the time R. W. Dixon's six-volume *History of the Church of England* from 1529 to 1570, especially vol. iv, is invaluable. More recently, Philip Hughes's three-volume *The Reformation in England,* especially vol. ii, should be read.

For Cranmer himself there is a wealth of material. The Parker Society has issued—I: *Writings and Disputations of Thomas Cranmer...relative to the Sacrament of the Lord's Supper* and II: *Miscellaneous Writings and Letters of Thomas Cranmer.* There is also Strype's *Memorials of Cranmer* and Jenkyns's *Remains of Thomas Cranmer.* These, with Gairdner's edition of *Bishop Cranmer's Recantacyons* provide a most complete index to Cranmer's theological mind. A modern exposition of Cranmer's intentions by an Anglican theologian is Gregory Dix's *The Shape of the Liturgy.*

A useful edition of Cranmer's two Prayer Books is the Everyman edition of *The First and Second Prayer Books of Edward VI* with an introduction by Bishop Gibson.

In the footnotes I have shortened to *Defence*, Cranmer's *The Defence of the True Catholic Doctrine of the Sacrament* (1550) and to *Reformatio* his new ecclesiastical code of 1553 *Reformatio Legum Ecelesiasticarum*.

PART II

The Great Betrayal

SOME THOUGHTS ON THE
INVALIDITY OF THE NEW MASS
(1970)

DEDICATION
*To the Roman Catholic Hierarchy
of England and Wales*

THE GOSPEL, THE "GOOD NEWS OF Jesus Christ," is the fact of the Resurrection. By rising from the dead, God Incarnate reversed the process of Nature and gave a new dimension to existence. Instead of death and decay, which seemed to be the inevitable end of all things, there was now seen to be Eternal Life.

The Apostles were the men who could bear firsthand witness to this unique phenomenon, who could say: "I saw Him and talked with Him and learnt from Him and touched Him and ate with Him after He had risen from the dead," men who went untroubled to their own deaths at the hands of unbelievers "in the sure and certain hope of resurrection."

Today, when to most people "gospel" means nothing more than one of the accounts of certain episodes in Christ's life, and "apostle" a peregrinatory white-bearded teacher of the first Christian century, it is almost impossible to realize the impact of this Good News of the abolition of death which was (and is) "to the Jews a stumbling-block and to the Greeks foolishness." Though it is the basis of the Christian faith, it is not even believed by a large body of nominal Christians who substitute for it a sentimental interest in social amelioration concern for *this* world on the principle that "death ends everything"—and pay only lip-service to the fact of Resurrection to eternal life.

Before He died and rose again, Christ had given His disciples the conditions for inheriting Eternal Life. He taught in the synagogue at Capernaum, the day after He had given a hint of the manner of the Eucharist-to-be by feeding five thousand people on five loaves and two small fishes which He had blessed; "Unless you eat My flesh and drink My blood, you have no life in you. Whoso eats My flesh and drinks My blood has Eternal Life and I will raise him up at the last day."

And from that time, it is recorded, many of His followers left Him, saying: "How can this man give us his flesh to eat?" The teaching was altogether too absurd! And there is at least this to be said for those pre-Crucifixion Protestants who deserted Him—that He had not explained the transubstantiation by which they were to be enabled to eat Him. That instruction was reserved for the twelve Apostles who were with Him in an upper room in Jerusalem the night before He was executed as a criminal. And when He took the bread and blessed it and said: "*This* is My Body" and the wine and said: "*This* is My Blood," there must surely have been, among other emotions, a sense of relief that His "hard saying" in the synagogue at Capernaum was at last made clear.

Some Thoughts on the Invalidity of the New Mass (1970)

From one point of view, the Church is the organization formed to protect the truth that the passport to Eternal Life is the Mass. Other sacraments can be seen as guarding the central one. In baptism, by symbolically and sacramentally sharing Christ's death, we become eligible for resurrection and, original sin obliterated, are in the state of purity necessary so that we do not "eat and drink to our own damnation." The sacrament of penance allows us, by absolution, to return to that state after we have committed actual sin. The sacrament of Holy Orders is the guarantee that the miracle of transubstantiation will be effected by a priest set apart for that purpose, who is in direct succession to the original Apostles and whose ministrations are thus valid.

In the centuries-long assault on the Church by the forces of evil, the attack has sometimes been directed at, so to speak, the "outworks" — at the Apostolic Succession or at Auricular Confession — but the main battle has eventually concentrated on the Mass.

In the earlier centuries, the heretical emphasis was on a denial of the Incarnation. The question whether the bread and wine became truly the Body and Blood was secondary to the question whether God had taken, or, indeed, could take — a human body. What may be called *the* heresy, because from the first century until today it has been the root of most of the other heresies, held that He could not have done so, because all matter was evil. Spirit, which was "good," could not inhabit flesh, which was "bad." This Gnosticism under various names troubled the Church from the very early years when Justin Martyr made "the Resurrection of the Body" the Christian battle-cry against the Gnostic "the immortality of the soul" and warned the faithful: "If you fall in with those who speak of the immortality of the soul, you will know they are not Christians."

The most dangerous and widespread recrudescence of Gnosticism was that in the Europe of the thirteenth century. It was then known as Catharism, the religion of "the Pure," and to save Christendom from this Puritanism, St. Dominic and his Order of Preachers fought it by argument and Simon de Montfort opposed it by an armed Crusade.

Though it was checked, it was not destroyed, and it handed on to later Puritanism the insistence that "matter" was "evil" and that transubstantiation was therefore not to be thought of. By isolating from its context a verse in the New Testament — "God is spirit and they that worship Him must worship Him in spirit and in truth" — the Puritans, then and now, implicitly denied the point that the uniqueness of Christianity is precisely that God is flesh which hung on a cross and rose from a tomb.

They could not, any more than their successors at the Reformation, get rid of a Communion service, because it was too well attested in Scripture; but they, again like their successors, emptied it of all orthodox meaning. The Cathar "consecration prayer" in their service of the Supper ran; "O Lord Jesus Christ, who didst bless the five loaves and two fishes in the wilderness and, blessing water, turned it into wine; bless, in the name of the Father, the Son and the Holy Spirit, this bread, fish and wine, not as a sacrifice or offering, but in simple commemoration of the Most Holy Supper of Jesus Christ and his disciples."

Here is the basis of all later heretical developments in the doctrine of the Eucharist, the repudiation of oblation and sacrifice.

One of the Church's replies to the menace of Catharism was the institution in 1285 of the recitation, by the priest, on his way back from the altar to the sacristy, of the Last Gospel. His genuflection at "the Word was made flesh" was the guarantee that he was not a secret Cathar and that in the Mass he had just celebrated his intention was to effect transubstantiation. Nor was the choice of the Prologue to St. John as the passage to be read irrelevant to the issue. This was originally a Gnostic hymn which had been Christianized by the interpolation of the historical verses referring to John the Baptist and Jesus and by the addition of "and the Word was made flesh," which destroyed the whole basis of the heresy.

When, after nearly 700 years the reading of the Last Gospel was abolished in 1965 on the ground that it was not in the "primitive rite" (how could it have been?) those with any knowledge of theology and history knew also that the heretical attack on the Mass had begun again in our days.

The Fourth Lateran Ecumenical Council, which met in 1215, was attended by 400 bishops, 800 abbots and priors and the representatives of the monarchs of Christendom. Its work included a definition of transubstantiation and a formal condemnation of the Cathars. Under its impetus, throughout the thirteenth century devotion to the Blessed Sacrament increased. The feast of Corpus Christi was instituted and given liturgical shape by St. Thomas Aquinas who wrote for it his famous hymns. Processions and, in the fourteenth century, Expositions of the Blessed Sacrament became popular.

But side by side with Catholic adoration there were increased heretical attacks. In England, John Wyclif, and in Bohemia his disciple, John Hus, denied that Christ's words meant what they said, and asserted that "This is My Body" Was to be interpreted in some such sense as "This means my body" — thus preparing the way for later Protestant ingenuity which in 1577 resulted in the publication of a book in Germany containing 200 different interpretations of the words "Hoc est Corpus Meum."

Some Thoughts on the Invalidity of the New Mass (1970)

Both Wyclif and Hus, while denying the Body and Blood, supported their central attack by subsidiary ones. Wyclif denied the Apostolic Succession and the right of priests to consecrate, by teaching that only "good" men could preside at the Supper; while Hus demanded communion in both kinds to contradict the orthodox doctrine that under the appearance of bread alone, as under the appearance of wine alone, we receive Christ whole and entire, because Christ is not divided so that in the Host we receive one part of Him and in the Chalice another. The purpose of the demand for "both kinds," then and now, was and is to deny the Sacrifice of the Mass and to assert the "memorial Supper."

* * *

In the sixteenth century, the anti-Catholic forces became grouped around the three great heresiarchs, Luther, Zwingli and Calvin. Although they taught different doctrines and referred to each other in unflattering terms, they were united in their hatred of the "never-sufficiently-to-be-execrated Mass." Adopting most of the Eucharistic heresies of the past and adding some new ones of their own, they led what is known as the Reformation.

Of the method of Archbishop Cranmer's destruction of the Mass in Protestant England, I have already written in *The Modern Mass*. Here the more relevant consideration is his conduct before his death in the reign of Mary Tudor when Catholicism was restored. Cranmer, with two other leading Protestants, Ridley and Latimer, asked to be allowed to debate the subject of transubstantiation with Catholic theologians. The request was granted and a public debate was held in Oxford on three propositions: 1) that, in the Eucharist, by virtue of Christ's words spoken by a priest, the Body and Blood of Christ are truly present under the forms of bread and wine: 2) that after the consecration there remains no substance of the bread and wine or any other substance but the Body and Blood; 3) and that the Mass is a Sacrifice, available to both the living and the dead for the propitiation of their sins.

After three days of argument, the Protestants were driven to repudiate the authority of the Lateran Council, "because it did not agree with God's Word." This attitude was, for them, a logical necessity, yet it took the Catholics, both those who were engaged in argument and the students and theologians who were listening, by surprise.

"What!" said the Prolocutor, "you do not acknowledge the Lateran Council?"

"No," said the Protestants, "we do not acknowledge it."

There was nothing more to be said, for this repudiation of what was undoubtedly the mind of Christendom was also a repudiation of the very idea of the development of the Church.

Some Thoughts on the Invalidity of the New Mass (1970)

As Karl Adam puts it in *The Spirit of Catholicism*: "Catholicism cannot be identified simply and wholly with primitive Christianity, in the same way that a great oak cannot be identified with the tiny acorn. There is no mechanical identity, but an organic identity. The Gospel of Christ would have been no living Gospel if it had remained for ever the tiny seed of A. D. 33 and had not struck root and grown up into a tree."

But this was the one thing that the sixteenth century Protestants could not admit and, to counter it, they used, if they did not actually invent, that absurd theory of history which one historian has actually called "Hunt the Acorn." That is to say, when you see a magnificent oak, you start to search for an acorn similar to that from which it grew and say: "Don't pay any attention to the tree, because this is what it ought to be like."

In addition to being so self-evidently silly — who would advocate, for instance, that the House of Commons should go back to being a Witanagemot and meet at Kingston-on-Thames? — this theory was also patently dishonest. It did not mean that primitive practice was followed in detail. It only meant that details were selected from primitive practice which were useful for discrediting contemporary custom.

It so happened that the Reformers found what they wanted in some early records. In the year 150 A. D. Justin Martyr wrote a letter to the Emperor Marcus

Aurelius in an effort to convince him that the Christians were not engaged in criminal activities at their service.

The conditions and surroundings of the Mass that Justin describes are those of a Church living daily under the shadow of persecution, and thus with everything reduced to a minimum of simplicity. His account is not likely, in fact, to be any more representative of the normal worship of the early Church than a letter written from an air-raid shelter in the middle of World War II would give a picture of normal life in twentieth century England.

But Justin's letter gave the Protestants the excuse they sought, and it had the additional advantage for them that it described the celebrant as the "president," since the use of the word "priest" would give the Emperor a wrong impression by its association with the pagan Roman priesthood.

On the basis of their absurd theory with its dishonest selectivity and its reliance on a single letter written on a particular occasion for a particular purpose, the Protestants invented their "true Christianity" and proceeded to have their Communion Service in the vernacular, to substitute a table for an altar, to make their churches as bare as possible, removing all statues, and to limit the Eucharist to a Memorial Meal in which the celebrant was a "president" who sat at the Table facing the people.

Because the Faithful had always been accustomed to the Mass as a Sacrifice, an equivocal phrase — "sacrifice of praise and thanksgiving," still used in the Anglican Prayer Book—was introduced to give the simple the impression that even in those strange new surroundings the Sacrifice was still acknowledged.

To meet the spread of heresy at the Reformation, an Ecumenical Council was again summoned. It met at Trent. It confirmed the decrees of the Fourth Lateran Council three centuries earlier and it promulgated others, so that the Tridentine definitions—from Tridentum, the Latin equivalent of Trent—still are the official formulation of the Catholic Faith.

On the main question of the Sacrifice of the Mass, it confirmed the age-long doctrine: "If any one says that the Mass is only a sacrifice of praise and thanksgiving but not a propitiatory Sacrifice; or that it profits only the recipient and that it ought not to be offered for the living and the dead for sins, punishments, satisfactions and other necessities, let him be anathema."

After the Council of Trent was over, Pope St. Pius V drew up a Roman Missal which should safeguard for the whole Church the so-much-attacked faith. There is no need for me to describe it, for it is the Missal that has been in general use until the beginning of Lent this year, 1970.

This Tridentine Mass was codified by St. Pius by his *Quo Primum* on July 19th, 1570.

"We determine and order by this our decree," wrote the saint, "to be valid in perpetuity that never shall anything be added to, omitted from or changed in this Missal. Specifically do we warn all persons in authority, of whatever dignity or rank, Cardinals not excluded, and command them as a matter of strict obedience never to use or permit any ceremonies or Mass prayers other than those contained in this Missal.

> At no time in the future can a priest ever be forced to use any other way of saying Mass. And in order once for all to preclude any scruples of conscience and fear of ecclesiastical penalties and censures, we declare herewith that it is by virtue of Our Apostolic Authority that we decree and prescribe that this present order of ours is to last in perpetuity and that never at a future date can it be revoked or legally amended.
>
> And if, nevertheless, anyone should ever dare attempt any action contrary to this order of ours, handed down for all time, let him know that he has incurred the wrath of Almighty God and of the blessed apostles, Peter and Paul.

And so the Tridentine Mass stood, a perpetual bulwark against heresy until, on April 3rd, 1969, the present Pope, Paul VI, in his Apostolic Constitution, *Missale Romanum*, set it aside to introduce in its place a vernacular Mass, conformable with the practice and principles

Some Thoughts on the Invalidity of the New Mass (1970)

of Protestantism, to be celebrated on a table by a priest facing the people and known as "the President."

The English reactions to the New Mass were immediate. The Pope's instruction appeared in translation on May 10th, 1969, and on May 17th the Latin Mass Society sent a petition to the Holy Father asking for a retention of the Tridentine Mass according to the Missal of St. Pius V. And when in September Cardinals Ottaviani and Bacci presented to the Pope a critical study of the New Mass prepared by a company of leading European theologians, pointing out that it "represents as a whole and in its details a striking departure from the Catholic theology of the Mass," the Latin Mass Society immediately made an English translation, and sent it personally to every bishop, priest and head of a religious Order in England.

The Hierarchy forbade priests to take any notice of the scholars' analysis, and the majority of the 7,000 copies went, presumably, straight into clerical wastepaper baskets.

In this important work, the theologians pointed out, with a wealth of scholarship, that: 1) the New Mass was substantially rejected by the Episcopal Synod; 2) had never been submitted to the collegial judgment of the Episcopal Conferences; 3) was never asked for by the people; 4) that it has every possibility of satisfying the most modernist of Protestants; 5) that, by a series of equivocations, it obsessively places the emphasis on the "supper" instead of the Sacrifice; 6) that no distinction is allowed to remain between Divine and human sacrifice; 7) that bread and wine are only "spiritually," not substantially, changed; 8) that the Real Presence of Christ is never alluded to and belief in it is implicitly repudiated; 9) that the position of both priest and people is falsified so that the celebrant appears as nothing more than a Protestant minister, while the true nature of the Church is intolerably misrepresented; 10) that the abandonment of Latin sweeps away finally all unity of worship and may have its effect on unity of belief; 11) and that, in any case, the New Order has no intention of standing for the Faith as taught by the Council of Trent to which the Catholic conscience is bound. In fact, it teems with insinuations or manifest errors against the purity of the Catholic religion and dismantles all defenses of the deposit of Faith.

The Vatican, as well as the English and Welsh Bishops, seem to have been presuming on a combination of theological ignorance and blind obedience to get the New Mass accepted without argument. They had done their best to avert suspicion by introducing the changes gradually. As Cardinal Heenan wrote in his Pastoral Letter of October 12th, 1969:

> Why does the Mass keep changing? Here is the answer. It would have been foolhardy to introduce all the changes at once. It was

Some Thoughts on the Invalidity of the New Mass (1970)

obviously wise to change gradually and gently. If all the changes had been introduced together, you would have been shocked.

The following month, Cardinal Heenan wrote as the foreword to the English translation of the New Mass:

> Wise Pope Paul VI has decided that the time has come to end experiments. He is satisfied that the form of the Mass will not need to be altered again in the foreseeable future . . . It is important to realize that the revision has been carried out under the Holy Father's personal supervision. There can be no question of its containing false doctrine.

This, of course, implies that whatever a Pope chooses to do or say is, *ipso facto*, right. Such an attitude to the Holy Father suggests a pagan oracle, rather than the Catholic teaching that a Pope is infallible only when speaking to the entire world on a question of faith and morals but that, in speaking to any audience less than the whole world and on any subject other than faith or morals, he is as fallible as anybody else.

The fallibility, indeed, is the safeguard of the infallibility; and to suppose that a Pope cannot and does not err is to expose the Faith to the kind of contemptuous criticism which led, for example, Lytton Strachey,[1]

---

1 Lytton Strachey (1880–1932), English author and critic. — Ed.

misunderstanding the doctrine of infallibility, to write:

> John XXII asserted in his Bull *Cum inter nonnullos* that the doctrine of the poverty of Christ was heretical. His predecessor, Nicholas III, had asserted in his Bull *Exiit qui seminat* that the doctrine of the poverty of Christ was the true doctrine, the denial of which was heresy. Thus, if John XXII was right, Nicholas III was a heretic. On the other hand, if John was wrong — well, he was a heretic. And in either case, what becomes of Papal Infallibility?

But, of course, Papal Infallibility is not in question here. There is only the conflict between two men, the truth of which is to be settled by the usual process of theological argument. In the same way, the setting aside by Paul VI of St. Pius V's ruling is a matter affording the Faithful a choice between the opinions of two men; and considering that St. Pius was defending Catholicism from the very Protestantism which, it cannot seriously be disputed, is inherent in the New Mass, the choice should not be too difficult. For, as Professor Gordon Rupp, one of the foremost Lutheran scholars, said at Cambridge on March 12th, 1970, speaking of the Vatican's reputed intention of quashing the excommunication of Luther: "It seems to be a logical step to take in view of the fact that the Vatican Council agreed with so much of Luther's theology for which he was condemned."

Some Thoughts on the Invalidity of the New Mass (1970)

Paul VI himself seems to have been surprised at the extent of the resistance to the New Mass, and on November 19th and 26th he made two allocutions, which were published in the English editions of *L'Osservatore Romano* for November 27th and December 4th, 1969. In them he defended the New Mass. He asserted that "the Mass of the New Rite remains the same Mass we have always had." He claimed that the new form was "Christ's Will," thus suggesting infallibility without claiming it. He explained that the changes were intended to draw worshippers "from their usual torpor" and "help to make the Mass a peaceful but demanding school of Christian sociology." He described Latin as "the language of the angels" and offered as a slight consolation to those ordinary people, who were no longer allowed to hear it as the nineteen-centuries-old language of the Mass, that it would still be used for "the Holy See's official acts." And he ordered: "Do not let us talk about the New Mass. Let us rather speak of the New Epoch in the Church's life."

At this point it is necessary to ask the question which is and must for long have been in everyone's mind: Why? We have all watched the Vatican's dismantling of the Faith with a growing sense of incredulity. This cannot be really happening. It must be a nightmare from which we shall shortly awake to find all the old sanctities untouched. In any case, why should the Pope and the Bishops act thus?

For the answer, we must make a short diversion into the subject of "ecumenism."

When Pope John XXIII on 25th January, 1959, announced "an Ecumenical Council," non-Catholics, according to Cardinal Bea (in an article published in 1961),

> ... thought that there was question of a Council which would bring together the representatives of all the Christian communities to discuss the question of unity. This interpretation was founded on the meaning of the word "ecumenical," used today to signify the coming together of all religious groups that call themselves Christian. This meaning of the term, to designate the representatives of all the Christian denominations, grew up together with the "ecumenical movement" and only in the last century. The misunderstanding was quickly cleared up.

The Cardinal was too optimistic. The misunderstanding was not cleared up. It is still not cleared up. Many still imagine that because Vatican II, like every General Council of the Church, was Ecumenical in the canonical sense (that is to say, composed of the Catholic bishops of the *oikoumene*, the world in communion with the Apostolic See), it was also "ecumenical" in the Protestant sense of the term.

Some Thoughts on the Invalidity of the New Mass (1970)

But Protestant ecumenism is a most deadly heresy. Not only is it indifferentism — any religion is as good as any other — but it denies the reality of the Church. It teaches that the True Church does not yet exist, but that it will come into being some time in the future by pooling the various "insights" of various Christian communities. The World Council of Churches, coordinating 239 sects, is its representative body.

The Catholic Church has, so far, resisted the pressure to commit the final apostasy of joining the World Council of Churches and, in so doing, proclaiming that it is just one among other churches, but, under Paul VI it has consented to send observers, and the Protestants were unofficially (in the sense of clandestinely) consulted in the making of the New Mass.

The activities of the World Council of Churches, aided by the continuing confusion between the classic Catholic use of Ecumenical and the Protestant "ecumenical movement," forced Vatican II, for the sake of clarification, to issue a decree on Ecumenism. In spite of a charity which might easily be mistaken for compromise, this document, if carefully examined, will be found to safeguard the Faith. It lays down that: 1) all Christian communities outside the Catholic Church are "defective;" 2) that "only through the Catholic Church of Christ can the means of salvation be reached in all their fullness;" 3) that "the unity bestowed by Christ on His Church at the beginning is still in existence in the Catholic Church;" 4) and that the Catholic Church alone possesses "the wealth of the whole of God's revealed truth and all the means of grace." It supports the great Encyclical of Pius XII on the nature of the Church, *Mystici Corporis*, which ruled that "only those are to be accounted really members of the Church who have been regenerated in the waters of baptism and profess the true faith and have not cut themselves off from the structure of the Body by their own unhappy act," (i.e. by being confirmed in a non-Catholic sect, and by insisting that "in itself baptism is only a beginning, an introduction . . . oriented to the complete profession of faith, the complete incorporation in the institute of salvation, as Christ wanted, the complete integration into the fellowship of the Eucharist."

De Œcumenisimo is thus a decree *against* the Protestant Ecumenical Movement, made necessary by the double-meaning of the word "ecumenical"; but the Dogmatic Constitution has become more and more disregarded as bishops invite heretics and schismatics to preach in Catholic pulpits, and encourage other activities which blur the distinctiveness of the Catholic Faith.

In particular, they tend to emphasize that baptism unites all Christians in the faith, but omit the equally important truth, laid down by *Mystici Corporis*, that the adult adherence to a non-Catholic sect breaks that

Some Thoughts on the Invalidity of the New Mass (1970)

relationship established by baptism, since "schism, heresy or apostasy are such of their very nature that they sever a man from the body of the Church."

As the Vatican appeared to move nearer to the World Council of Churches, it became necessary to bring the New Mass into line with Protestant ecumenism; and for this purpose the very words of consecration said by Christ Himself were altered. Instead of saying that His blood was to be shed "for many," He was made to say "for all." This evil and dangerous doctrine of "the final salvation of all mankind," so absolutely at variance with the Church's teaching and so opposed to the clear teaching of Christ Himself, is the actual cornerstone of the whole edifice of heresy promoted today under the guise of "ecumenism."[2]

Heretical attempts had been made in earlier centuries to substitute "all" for "many" and they had been condemned by St. Thomas Aquinas himself. The alteration contradicts Christ's words at the Last Supper: "Lord, I pray not for the world, but for those whom thou has given me . . . neither pray I for these alone but for them also who shall believe in me through their word" — the prayer defining the exclusive nature of the Church. The World is saved by coming into the Church

---

[2] This quotation is from Patrick Henry Omlor's essay, "The Ventriloquists" (*Interdum*, 24 February 1970) to which I am indebted for the facts about Dr. Jeremias which follow.

and all men, of course, have that chance of salvation. But not all men take it. By their own free wills, they exclude themselves. The substitution of "all" for "many" fosters the ecumenical idea that all men's sins will be forgiven, regardless of creed or character.

The history of the alteration is instructive. The Pope, in his allocution of 19th November, 1969, to which I referred earlier, announced that the changes "had been thought out by authoritative experts of sacred liturgy." He omitted to mention that among those consulted were two Anglicans, a Lutheran, a Calvinist and a representative of the World Council of Churches, or that the expert responsible for the "all" was Dr. Joachim Jeremias, a non-Catholic professor at the University of Göttingen, who has attacked the Divinity of Christ.

Dr. Jeremias, in his book *The Eucharistic Words of Jesus*, published in 1966, invented the ingenious theory that when Christ said "for many" He meant "for all," because Aramaic does not possess any word meaning "all." Thus, the argument was transferred from theology, which, since the Council of Trent had expressly rejected and repudiated "for all men," was dangerous ground even for skilled equivocators, to philology.

However, the argument was quite unsound. Not only does the passage: "All the inhabitants of the earth are reputed as nothing" (Daniel IV, 32) exist in the original Aramaic, but *A Grammar of Biblical Aramaic*

Some Thoughts on the Invalidity of the New Mass (1970)

(published in 1961) devotes an entire section to the Aramaic word for "all," "everybody," and "everyone."

The "official" explanation of this particular point in the New Mass is, like so many of them, what the simple man, unacquainted with episcopal methods of thought, would call a lie. Its importance here is that, in altering the words of Christ, *it surely makes every vernacular Mass invalid*, beyond any possibility of argument.

As the Latin versions of the new Canons of the Mass still retain "*pro multis*" and have not yet changed it to "*pro omnibus*," this easily-seen reason for invalidity does not apply to them. They, however, seem none the less invalid, but before examining the reason it may be well to say a word about the Canon of the Mass, because our ecclesiastical authorities are misleading the laity by pretending that it is no more than 400 years old.

The way in which the change has been presented to the English may be summarized by Cardinal Heenan's sentence in the Foreword to the Westminster Mass Book. "Words and actions which, four hundred years ago, appealed to the Elizabethans can hardly meet the mood of men in the twentieth century."

But, on the contrary, the Canon of the Mass goes back without any alteration at all to the early Christian centuries. It was already established before St. Augustine brought Christianity to Britain, and the Canon he used in the first Mass he said in Kent consisted of precisely the same words in the same language as have been used in every Mass said in the 1,373 years between then and the abolition of it in February, 1970.

What the Tridentine reform of St. Pius V revised and unified were occasional prayers and rituals which had grown up in certain localities. It did not touch — as they had not touched — the Canon, which had the changelessness of Christ.

Trent itself stressed the continuance. "The Catholic Church," it declared, "in order that the Holy Sacrifice may be offered in a dignified and reverent way, established the sacred Canon centuries ago, so pure and free from all error that nothing is contained in it which does not, in the greatest way, inspire, sanctify and raise the mind to God."

Luther, on the other hand, spoke of it as "that abominable Canon which is a confluence of slimy puddles. They have made of the Mass a sacrifice. They have added offertories. The Mass is not a sacrifice. It is not the act of a sacrificing priest. With the Canon, we discard all that implies an oblation." One of the chief architects of the New Mass, Rev. Annibale Bugnini, appears to endorse this judgment when he speaks of Luther's famous *Formula Missæ* of 1523 as a *Missa Normativa*. Certainly the design of the New Mass, with its destruction of the age-old Canon, embodies Lutheran principles.

Some Thoughts on the Invalidity of the New Mass (1970)

As long as the Tridentine Canon remained, it was impossible to subvert the intention of the Mass. Consequently, the ecumenists had to impose alternative Canons. One of these, Canon II, was framed in such a way that any Protestant minister or lapsed priest who denied transubstantiation could say it.

First of all, it got rid of all mention of oblation, as Luther had recommended. The reason for this is explained simply by a theologian in the *Courrier de Rome* (No. 49, p. 6): "As Christ rose from the dead to die no more, He cannot in the Mass be put in any state whatever of a victim. He can only be the Victim mystically under the species of bread and wine. The bread and wine come in, therefore, as integral parts of the Sacrifice."

Having got rid of the offertory, and the Oblations set apart, the compilers of Canon II fell back on Cranmer's trick in framing a prayer not that the bread and wine might be made the Body and Blood, but that "they may be *unto us*[3] the body and blood" — a formula which he described as intended specifically to deny transubstantiation.

So, in Canon II, the formula, "Let your spirit come upon these gifts to make them holy so that they may

---

[3] It is true that the Tridentine Canon also contains *nobis*, but, because of the great oblationary prayers which precede, the meaning is quite different. See Part I of this volume, *The Modem Mass*, p. 30–31.

become for us the body and blood of our Lord Jesus Christ," makes it possible for any of the member sects of the World Council of Churches to use it as their communion service. This "ecumenical" intention surely destroys its validity.

Also, the validity of the other Canons would thus appear to be equally destroyed.

I have heard people say that, because Father So-and-So undoubtedly believes in transubstantiation, his celebration will, because of his intention, be valid. This is to misunderstand "intention." The personal belief of the priest has no part in it. If it had, the fact that Talleyrand was a professed atheist would have invalidated all his ordinations and there would be today no certain orders anywhere in France. What is asked of the priest is simply that he should intend what the Church intends. This principle explains, for example, why a Muslim woman could perform a valid Christian baptism, provided she says the appointed words, does the appointed actions and, though herself disbelieving, intends to do what the Church intends.

As the Church has, by framing Canon II so that it can be construed to deny transubstantiation, made its "ecumenical" intention incontrovertibly clear, it seems to follow that all the new Canons are invalid and that no priest, however sound his theology and however passionate his devotion, *can* say a valid Mass.

Some Thoughts on the Invalidity of the New Mass (1970)

So stark and appalling a conclusion has presented the great body of the faithful with an almost intolerable strain. It has even led some to the conclusion that an invalid Mass is valid if only it is said in Latin. They have formed an Association for Latin Liturgy, against which the faithful should be warned, not because it has any standing, but because the Hierarchy, to the further confusion of the simple, might seem to patronize it by appearing to grant a Latin Mass.

It cannot be too much emphasized that there is no certainly valid Latin Mass available in the West at the moment but the Tridentine Rite of St. Pius V, which he tried to safeguard in perpetuity.

Our bishops, forbidding this rite, call on our "obedience." But they must surely know that obedience to conscience takes precedence of everything, and that obedience cannot be commanded for something wrong. Even in military life, a soldier can no longer plead obedience to a superior as an excuse for committing a crime. What the bishops mean by "obedience" is mindless regimentation — the kind of obedience which the apostate priests of the first Reformation gave to their apostate bishops, among whom there was only one who defended the Faith — St. John Fisher. At the moment, there is no St. John Fisher.

The defense of the Church, in the face of the great betrayal by the ecclesiastics, devolves on the laity, who should be active in pursuing the policy which is already coming into effect in various places—providing a priest to say the Tridentine Mass and devoting to his upkeep all the money they would normally give to their local church. As we are back to the Catacombs, the celebration can be held in private houses.

There can be no possible censures for this. It was for this eventuality that St. Pius decreed: "At no time in the future can a priest ever be forced to use any other way of saying Mass." It would, in the end, be impossible to accuse of schism those who continued to use the form of Mass sanctified by the centuries. It is the ecumenists who would be the schismatics.

Some may feel that this course, by possibly reducing the numbers of the Church, is, for that reason, open to the gravest objections. They tend to think of events in terms of the line from the hymn, "Like a mighty army moves the Church of God," and see it as growing all the time numerically stronger.

But because the Gospel must indeed be preached to the whole world, it by no means follows that the whole world will receive it. If there is one thing on which Christ Himself, the Apostles and the Fathers insisted, it was that the Church on Earth will be reduced to a very small remnant. We have been warned on the highest authority of a "falling away," that "the time will come when they will not endure sound doctrine," and that

Some Thoughts on the Invalidity of the New Mass (1970)

"if it were possible the very elect" will be deceived.

An American priest, Father Lawrence Brey (1927–2008), writing of our present condition, asks whether the introduction of the New Mass is... the beginning of an age of new darkness on the Earth and the harbinger of an unprecedented crisis within the Church? Was the Blessed Virgin's indication that the Rosary and her Immaculate Heart would be our "last and final weapons" a hint that somehow the Holy Mass would at some point become no longer available to most Catholics?

Now that this has happened, some people, pending the organization of Tridentine Masses, say the Rosary followed by the reading of the Mass in their old missals, accompanied by an unfaltering, even passionate, intention to make a communion of desire, since they can no longer make one in fact. One can only pray that the days of this improvised necessity will, by God's grace, be shortened.

In conclusion, I must insist that this necessity in England is entirely the doing of our bishops. The Tridentine Mass, by the Pope's order, is not to be generally abolished until November 1971, unless the local Hierarchy chooses to forbid it. If our episcopate were to restore, or permit the alternative use of, the Tridentine Mass until Advent 1971, so that the matter could be thoroughly examined and debated, it is possible that it would not be abolished at all. Eighteen months of honesty might work wonders.

As a last word, may I commend to the Hierarchy of England and Wales the words with which Father Messenger concluded his review of a book on Anglican Orders almost as full of *suppressio veri* and *suggestio falsi* as various episcopal pronouncements on the New Mass: "I would appeal to the author to take this matter more seriously, not only for his own sake but for that of others also. It is a serious thing to deceive and delude souls for whom Christ died.

London, Palm Sunday 1970

LIST OF BOOKS
BY THE AUTHOR

The Poetry of T. S. Eliot (1932)
John Hampden: A Life (1933)
Rose and Glove: A Play (1934)
After the Event: A play in One Act (1935)
King James I (1935)
Gods and Mortals in Love (1936)
The Seven Deadly Virtues; In a Glass Darkly; Various Heavens: A Play Sequence (1936)
Cinderella's Grandchild: A Play in One Act (1936)
Mr Gladstone: A Play in Three Acts (1937)
Stories from History: Ten Plays for Schools (1938)
Who is for Liberty? (1939)
George Villiers, First Duke of Buckingham: Study for a Biography (1940)
A. D. 33: A Tract for the Times (1941)
Captain Thomas Schofield (1942)
Paul, A Bond Slave: A Radio Play (1945)
Charles and Cromwell (1946)
The Arrow and the Sword: An Essay in Detection (1947)
Queen Elizabeth: A Play in Three Acts (1947)
The Story Without an End (A collection of 33 radio broadcasts on the life of Christ) (1947)
Were You There...?: Six Meditations for Holy Week (1947)
The Silver Bowl (1948)
The Seven Christian Virtues (1949)

Four Stuart Portraits (1949)
The Evidence for the Gunpowder Plot (1950)
The Gunpowder Plot (1951)
Sir Walter Raleigh (1951)
Conversation with a Ghost (1952)
Jeremy Taylor (1952)
The Ancient Capital: An Historian in Search of Winchester (1953)
Canterbury Cathedral (1953)
The Children's Book of British Saints (1953)
His Eminence of England: A Play in Two Acts (1953)
The Children's Book of French Saints (1954)
The Children's Book of Italian Saints (1955)
The Great Prayer: Concerning the Canon of the Mass (1955)
James: By the Grace of God (1955)
Historical Whodunits (1955)
The Walled Garden: An Autobiography (1956)
The Beginning of the English Reformation (1957)
Enigmas of History (1957)
The Day They Killed the King (1957)
The Challenge of Bernadette (1958)
The Children's Book of German Saints (1958)
The Sisters (1958)
The Children's Book of Patron Saints (1959)
The Conspirators and the Crown (1959)
Young People's Book of the Saints (1960)
A Wicked Pack of Cards (1961)
Teresa of Avila: A Play (1961)
The Day Shakespeare Died (1961)

List of Books by the Author

The Flowering Hawthorn (1962)
Guy Fawkes (1964)
The Modern Mass: A Reversion to the Reforms of Cranmer (1969)
The Great Betrayal (1970)

THE PASSING OF THE PLANTAGENETS SERIES:
The Butt of Malmsey (1967)
The Marriage Made in Blood (1968)
A Matter of Martyrdom (1969)
The Cardinal in Exile (1969)
The Cardinal in England (1970)

THE LAST OF THE VALOIS SERIES:
The Florentine Woman (1970)
The Last of the Valois (1971)
Paris is Worth a Mass (1971)

Kind Kit: An Informal Biography of Christopher Marlowe (1972)
Catherine de' Medici (1973)
Letter to Julia (1974)
Lorenzo the Magnificent (1974)
Historical Enigmas (1974)
The Princess a Nun!: A Novel Without Fiction (1978)

www.ingramcontent.com/pod-product-compliance
Lightning Source LLC
Chambersburg PA
CBHW021429070526
44577CB00001B/130

* 9 7 8 1 9 8 9 9 0 5 8 2 1 *